PASSIVE INCOME IDEAS: ULTIMATE GUIDE DROPSHIPPING - E-COMMERCE BUSINESS AND MORE THAN 20 DIFFERENT WAYS THAT YOU CAN GENERATE PASSIVE INCOME

Adam Diesel

Cover design by: Art Painter
Library of Congress Control Number: 2018675309
Printed in the United States of America

I Want to thank you and congratulate you for buying my book
Passive Income Ideas: Ultimate Guide
Dropshipping - E-commerce business
and more than 20 different ways that
you can generate passive income

CONTENTS

Introduction

Everyone dreams of having a steady stream of passive income, but often wonder where to start. Well, look no further! Here are ideas to help you get started and create lucrative passive income streams. Whether you're just starting out or have been earning income through passive sources for years, this article will give you valuable insight into ways to make money without actively working for it. From setting up a side business to savvy investments, these strategies can provide long-term financial stability and success.

Passive Income Ideas can help you create a steady stream of money without having to work for it. Passive income requires minimal effort and maintenance on your part. Investing in rental properties, dividend stocks, high-yield savings accounts, and peer-to-peer lending are all great examples of how passive income can be earned. In addition, passive income can be earned from a variety of sources and doesn't require you to leave your home.

CHAPTER 1: WHAT IS THE MEANING OF PASSIVE INCOME?

Passive income is an income stream where money is earned without actively working for it. Passive income can come from investments, rental properties, online businesses, or other sources that require minimal maintenance effort. Passive income can provide a consistent source of revenue and help you achieve financial stability over the long-term.

What Is The Meaning Of Active

Income?

Active income is a form of income that requires the recipient to regularly perform some kind of activity in order to earn money. This includes things like wages, salaries, and tips from jobs, businesses or freelancing activities. It also includes any other type of income where someone has to put in time, effort and sometimes even capital before they can earn money. Active income is also known as earned income, and it's often contrasted with passive income. Passive income does not require active effort; the money comes in without additional work after the initial investment or set-up.

Compared to passive income, active income is much more labor intensive and there are significant risks associated with it. There is no guarantee that you will earn money with active income, and if the business or job ends up failing, your income source may be gone. Despite this, many people prefer active income because of the earning potential and satisfaction they get from working hard to achieve their goals. It can also provide financial security by helping you cover monthly basic living expenses.

Overall, active income is an important part of many people's lives, providing them with a steady source of income that can help them make ends meet and pursue their goals. While some risks are associated with it, it can also be very rewarding when you put in the effort and make the most of your opportunities.

Upfront Investment

When embarking on any project or business venture, it's important to consider the upfront investment required. The upfront investment isn't just limited to financial costs - it can also refer to resources and time necessary for success.

Before committing to a project, take into account what kind of resources you'll need - whether they be financial, such as cash, or non-financial, such as personnel and materials. Make sure you have a solid plan for how to finance the upfront costs, including any interest rates associated with financing.

Additionally, it's important to consider the time investment required. Upfront investments can be substantial, and if realized over long periods, they can become even more expensive. Make sure you factor it will take to implement your project fully and that you are able to commit for the duration.

Finally, make sure you have a realistic expectation of what kind of return on investment (ROI) can be expected from your upfront investments. Upfront investments should only be made when there is a realistic expectation of recouping costs soon.

By taking into account all of these factors, you'll

be best prepared to make an informed decision about whether or not to commit to an upfront investment. Upfront investments can provide great opportunities for success, but only if done right.

Short-Term Income

refers to income earned in the short-term, usually within a one-year time frame. Short-term income is typically earned through employment, investments, or other sources of regular payments. Short-term income can be used to cover costs associated with daily living expenses such as food and housing, but it can also be used for larger purchases such as a car or home. Short-term income can also be used to build up savings, put toward investments, or give to charity. Short-term income is a key part of financial stability, allowing individuals to pay bills and build wealth on their own terms. Understanding how to increase short-term income can help individuals make the most of their financial future.

One way to increase short-term income is to increase one's earning potential by taking on additional jobs or roles. This may involve taking on extra shifts at work, finding freelance projects online, or exploring new opportunities in the gig economy. Short-term investments are another way to boost income and can include investing in stocks, bonds, and cryptocurrencies. Investing in real estate can also increase short-term income, as rental properties can generate a steady stream of monthly payments. Finally, individuals may consider taking out a loan to cover expenses or start a business venture with the potential to create more long-term financial stability.

With careful planning and strategic thinking, individuals can increase their short-term income and reap the rewards of financial stability. Short-term income is a valuable resource that can be used to cover day-to-day expenses, build long-term savings, or invest in future opportunities. Increasing one's short-term income takes time and effort, but it can lead to greater financial stability and a more secure future.

Long-Term Income

is an essential part of a successful financial plan. By investing money towards long-term goals, consumers can ensure that their future is secure and that retirement is taken care of. Achieving this kind of stability requires careful planning, research and understanding of how different kinds of investments work together to achieve the best possible outcome.

The most effective way to build long-term income is through a diversified portfolio of investments, including stocks, bonds and other securities. The key is to create a balance between risk and reward that meets

individual needs and goals. For example, an investor who wishes to build long-term income should consider investing in both aggressive and conservative investments and allocating a portion of their portfolio to fixed-income investments, such as bonds and cash equivalents.

Investors should also think about how to best manage their portfolios over time by periodically rebalancing their investments to ensure that they are still on track to meet long-term goals. Additionally, investors should consider the tax implications of their investments and periodically review their portfolio to ensure that it is meeting their financial objectives and that they aren't missing any opportunities.

Finally, investors should stay informed about the latest market developments so they can adjust their portfolios when needed. By staying on top of current trends, investors can maximize their chances of achieving long-term income.

Short-Term Profits

Short-Term Profits are a type of financial gain that can be realized quickly. Short-term profits are usually the result of an investment with the expectation to receive a return within a relatively short period, often weeks or months. Short-term investments are typically less risky than long-term investments since they provide an immediate return and require less analysis of future market conditions. Short-term profits can come from the sale of stocks or other investments such as real estate, bonds, commodities and currencies. Short-term profits are often used to meet near-term financial obligations or increase a business's liquidity. Short-term profits are also useful for diversifying an investor's portfolio and keeping it balanced while waiting for long-term investments to pay off. Short-term profits can be a beneficial strategy, but they also come with risks and investors should weigh the advantages and disadvantages of investing in this manner.

Short-term profits are not only sought by individual investors, but also businesses. Short-term profits help businesses meet their goals quickly while they continue to pursue long-term objectives. Short-term profits are generated by taking advantage of opportunities in the market, such as buying and selling goods or services at competitive prices. Short-term profits can also be achieved through cost-cutting measures that eliminate excess expenses without negatively impacting the operation of the business. Short-term profits may only sometimes be possible to achieve, but they can provide a valuable alternative when appropriately used.

Short-term profits can help businesses maintain their financial stability while achieving a competitive edge in the market. Short-term profits are also important for investors seeking to diversify their portfolios or increase liquidity to meet near-term obligations. Short-term profits can be easily realized, but they come with risks and should always be weighed carefully. Short-term profits are an important part of any successful financial strategy.

Long-Term Profits

Long-Term Profits are a key aspect of running a successful business. Long-term profits are the result of consistent and well-planned investments, as well as strategic executions that guarantee the longevity of a company. Long-term profits can be achieved through a variety of methods ranging from smart investments to developing quality products and services that meet customer needs. Long-term profits are essential for businesses to remain competitive and maximize their potential in the market. Long-term profits allow companies to diversify their income streams and provide a stable source of revenue that can be used to invest in new initiatives, research, and development. Long-term profits also enable companies to plan for the future and fund growth, enabling them to achieve sustained success. Ultimately, long-term profits are essential for businesses to remain profitable and competitive in the long run.

Understanding the importance of Long-Term Profits is essential for both established and startup business owners. Established businesses should focus on optimizing their current strategies while also planning ahead for future growth and opportunities. Startups should ensure that their investments are planned with Long-Term Profits in mind from the outset to ensure that their projects remain profitable over time. Long-term profits can drive growth and success, so understanding them is crucial for any business's longevity.

The key to achieving Long-Term Profits is knowing when to take risks and when to play it safe. Long-term profits should be viewed as a long-term goal, meaning businesses should focus on more than immediate results. Long-term profits require strategic investments, careful planning, and the ability to anticipate and adapt to changes in the market. Investing in equipment or technology with a longer lifespan can also help businesses reach Long-Term Profits, as can partnerships and collaborations with other companies. Long-term profits also depend on how well a business understands its customers and is able to meet their needs over time.

Ultimately, Long-Term Profits are essential for businesses to remain competitive and maximize their potential in the market. Therefore, a Long-Term understanding of Profits is essential, and businesses should plan strategically and invest wisely in order to reach Long-Term Profits. With careful planning and a focus on understanding customer needs, Long-Term Profits can be reached and sustained over time.

Long-Term profits are an important part of running a successful business. Companies should focus on long-term investments and understand Long-Term Profits to achieve sustained market success. Long-term profits should be viewed as a long-term goal, with businesses planning ahead for future growth and opportunities. Businesses must anticipate and adapt to changes in the market while also understanding customer needs in order to reach Long-Term Profits. With Long-Term Profits, businesses can secure a long-term source of income and plan for sustained growth. Long-Term Profits are essential for companies to remain competitive and maximize their potential in the market.

Advantage Of Passive Income Ideas

One of the main advantages of passive income ideas is that they require minimal upfront effort. Unlike traditional jobs, where you have to invest time and energy into performing specific tasks, passive income can be generated without much hard work or commitment. This makes them attractive to those who are looking for ways to make money without having to devote a lot of their time and energy.

Another advantage of passive income ideas is that they can generate a steady stream of additional income. As long as you are consistent in your efforts and choose the right strategies, you can make money from passive sources on a regular basis. This extra income can supplement your current salary or cover living expenses, giving you the financial freedom to pursue your dreams.

Passive income ideas can provide a sense of security and independence. Being able to generate money without relying on an employer or other income source allows you to build your own future without worrying about how you will pay for it. This peace of mind can be invaluable in helping you stay motivated and focused on achieving your goals.

You're Not Reliant On A Paycheck

When it comes to generating passive income, one of the biggest advantages is that you are not relying solely on a paycheck. You have multiple sources of income, which can provide financial security and stability. You don't need to worry about your employer cutting hours or laying off employees. You can make money while you sleep, even if you're not actively working on your business. You can generate a steady stream of income from your passive income ideas, even if the economy is down or you're facing other challenges. You don't have to be at the mercy of an employer for your financial security. You are free to pursue your passions and make money doing it. With passive income ideas, you can achieve financial freedom and stability. You don't have to worry about relying on a single paycheck or being at the mercy of an employer. You can control your finances and make money while still pursuing your passions. With passive income ideas, the sky is the limit! You can create multiple sources of income and achieve financial freedom. You can make money while you sleep and still pursue your passions without worrying about relying solely on a paycheck. You're in control of your destiny and can create a secure future with the right passive income ideas.

Gain Additional Cash Flow

Gain additional cash flow with passive income ideas. Passive income is a great option for those looking to make money outside of their job or build up a retirement fund. Passive income is an income that requires little to no active work from the owner. It can be made through investments, rental properties, or business ownership. The advantage of passive income is that it allows you to make money without having to work long hours or put in a lot of effort.

Overall, passive income ideas offer a variety of advantages that make them appealing to those who are looking for ways to supplement their incomes or achieve financial independence. From minimal upfront investment to steady streams of additional money and increased security and freedom, these strategies can be an excellent way for you to reach your short-term and long-term goals.

The Disadvantages Of Passive Income Ideas

disadvantages of passive income ideas are numerous. First, the income generated from these ideas can be unpredictable and unreliable. Even if you have an excellent idea, there is no guarantee that it will generate any income or that it will remain consistent in the long term. Additionally, passive income sources often require a significant amount of upfront capital to get them up and to run. This can make it difficult to generate any income at all, and consistent and reliable income. Finally, passive income ideas may require more time and effort than anticipated to be successful. This is especially true for those who need an extensive understanding of the business or industry in which they are investing their money. For these reasons, it is important to do your research before investing in any passive income idea. With sufficient knowledge and preparation, you can be sure to increase your chances of success. However, there is always the risk that you may not generate any investment return. Therefore, weighing the pros and cons before committing to a passive income idea is important. By researching and understanding the risks, you can make an informed decision that is in line with your goals. With the right approach, passive income ideas can be beneficial, but it's important to remember that there are also potential downsides. It's best to take time to understand all the details involved and plan accordingly before taking the plunge. This will help to ensure that you're making an informed decision and setting yourself up for success in the long term. In this way, passive income ideas can be a great way to build wealth – as long as you do your due diligence.

Is Passive Income Taxed?

The answer to this question is yes. Passive income is subject to taxation similarly to other forms of income, including wages and capital gains. However, the tax rate applied to passive income depends on the type of income and the individual's personal circumstances. For example, certain types of businesses may be subject to special taxation, while some investments may be eligible for lower tax rates. Additionally, certain deductions and credits may apply, which can reduce the amount of tax owed on passive income. Ultimately, it is important to understand the tax implications for any form of passive income to ensure that the right amount of tax is paid. It is also important to note that passive income may be subject to self-employment taxes in some cases, so it is important to understand the rules in order to determine whether or not taxes are due.

CHAPTER 2 :WHAT ARE THE DIFFERENT TYPES OF PASSIVE INCOME?

C reating passive income is an effective way to generate long-term wealth. Some examples of passive income include rental properties, dividend stocks, royalties from creative works like books or music, peer-to-peer lending, and business opportunities. Creating a passive income requires some upfront work to get set up, but once in place, the income will continue to come in with minimal effort required. Creating a passive income stream can be an excellent way to build long-term wealth and financial security. By diversifying your income sources and creating multiple streams of passive income, you can be well on your way to achieving financial freedom. With patience and dedication, anyone can create a passive income that will help them reach their financial goals.

Investing

Investing is one of the most popular sources of passive income. Investing in stocks, bonds, mutual funds, and other financial instruments can generate a steady income stream. Investing in real estate is another popular form of passive income, as it can generate rental income or capital gains if the property appreciates in value. Investing in a business, such as through franchising or angel investing, can also be a great way to generate passive income. Investing in dividend-paying stocks or passive index funds can also provide a steady income stream. Finally, starting an online business can be a great way to generate passive income. With an online business, you can use a variety of digital marketing strategies, such as content marketing and affiliate marketing, to generate income.

What Are The Skills That You Need?

Building passive income streams requires a certain set of skills. First, you must understand the different passive income sources, such as investments, real estate, royalties and business opportunities. As different sources require different amounts of work and risk, it is important to understand the benefits and drawbacks of each.

Another important skill is the ability to save money and invest it wisely. If you have a tight budget, it's important to be able to identify where you can save money, so that you have enough capital available for investing.

Having good financial management skills is also important because it helps you to manage your investments and make informed decisions. This includes understanding taxes, accounting, budgeting and investing strategies.

Finally, having a good understanding of marketing and sales can help you to generate more passive income streams. Most businesses need some form of advertising to gain customers, and a basic understanding of marketing can help you create effective strategies. Good sales skills can also help you monetize your ideas more effectively.

How To Improve Your Ability To Save

Money?

The key to passive income is to have the ability to save money. To do this, you need to develop skills and habits. First, you need to be disciplined in how you spend money. This means avoiding unnecessary purchases and focusing on the value of your money.

You also need to be able to budget effectively. This means setting and sticking to limits on how much money you spend each month to save more money.

Finally, it is important to develop good financial planning skills. This means understanding how taxes, investments and other financial instruments work, so that you can make smart decisions about how to allocate your resources for the best possible return on investment. Knowing how to manage risks is also essential for developing passive income streams.

By developing these skills and putting them into practice, you can start to build up a steady stream of passive income and become more financially secure.

Financial Planning Skills

Financial planning skills are essential for anyone trying to create passive income. To be successful, you need to know how to accurately forecast

future cash flows and create financial plans that account for changes in the market. You also need to have a good understanding of taxes and how they will affect your earnings. Finally, you should understand basic investment principles so that you can make sound investments to grow your passive income. Strong financial planning skills are key to achieving long-term success in creating passive income. Investing the time and effort into further developing these skills can pay off big in the future as you start to reap the benefits of your hard work. With a little bit of knowledge and persistence, anyone can create a steady stream of passive income. All you need to do is take the time to understand the basics and develop your financial planning skills. Investing in yourself will pay off big in the long run. The better your financial literacy, the more successful you will be at creating passive income!

Understanding Of Marketing And Sales

understanding of marketing and sales are essential skills needed to generate passive income. Understanding these two concepts is key to successfully creating and maintaining a steady source of passive income. Marketing involves creating effective campaigns targeting the right audience and understanding what your potential customers need or want. Sales require understanding how to close sales effectively and understanding the customer's journey from understanding their problem to the solution you offer. It can be difficult to create a successful passive income stream without understanding both of these aspects. Furthermore, understanding how to effectively market and sell your product or service is key to increasing revenue and growing your business. Understanding marketing and sales are essential for creating a successful passive income stream.

CHAPER 3 :PASSIVE INCOME IDEA

Peer-to-peer lending
Peer-to-peer lending is a revolutionary new way of borrowing and lending money, cutting out the middlemen like traditional banks and financial institutions. Peer-to-peer lending allows individual borrowers and lenders to connect directly with one another in an online marketplace, allowing for more efficient and secure transactions than ever before. Peer-to-peer loans are typically offered at lower interest rates than those offered by traditional banks, making them an attractive option for both borrowers and lenders. Additionally, peer-to-peer loans can be used for various purposes, including business investments, buying a home or car, or

even consolidating debt. Peer-to-peer lending has revolutionized the way people access funding and made it easier for borrowers to find the financing they need for their projects. Peer-to-peer loans offer a fast, secure and low-cost way of accessing capital, allowing borrowers to take advantage of some of the best rates available on the market. Peer-to-peer lending can provide a great alternative to traditional banking systems, especially for those with bad credit or who cannot secure a loan from a traditional lender. Peer-to-peer lending is quickly becoming one of the most popular ways for individuals to access capital and can be an invaluable asset when it comes to financing projects and investments.

What Are The Steps For Starting Peer-To-Peer Lending?

The first step to starting Peer-to-peer (P2P) lending is to create an account on a reputable P2P lending platform. This can be done online and generally requires basic personal information such as name, address, and email address. After registering for the platform, users must then verify their identity via KYC processes, such as providing a government-issued ID.

The second step is to create an investment profile, which will allow the P2P lending platform to recommend suitable investments for you. This will include setting your risk appetite and desired return goals. The platform can match borrowers with lenders based on their criteria with this information.

The third step is to fund your account. This can be done by linking the platform to a bank or debit/ credit card, transferring money from a digital wallet, or using cryptocurrency. The minimum amount of funds that must be deposited varies by P2P lending platform and is usually between $50-$100.

Once these steps have been completed, users can begin searching for potential investments. Users can specify criteria such as loan type, interest rate, and repayment terms when searching. As borrowers apply for loans on the platform, users can review their profiles and decide if they want to invest in that particular loan.

By following these steps, Peer-to-peer lending can be a simple and effective way to invest money and generate passive income. With the right platform and diligent research, P2P lending can be a great way to diversify your portfolio. However, it is important to remember to always review potential investments carefully before making any decisions. Additionally, it's essential to stay up-to-date on all relevant laws for Peer-to-peer lending in your area. Doing so can help ensure peer-to-peer lending is a safe, profitable, and enjoyable experience.

Advantage Of Peer-To-Peer Lending As Passive Income

Peer-to-peer lending offers an attractive opportunity to make money with very little effort. Peer-to-Peer (P2P) lending is becoming a popular way of investing, as it can provide higher yields than more traditional investments such as stocks and bonds. Investors earn interest on their loans, while borrowers benefit from lower rates compared to those offered by banks and other traditional lenders. P2P lending is often seen as a way of passive income, as it requires minimal effort to set up, allowing investors to earn money without having to take on any active management or maintenance responsibility. Peer-to-Peer lending can also be an attractive investment for those looking to diversify their portfolios. As with any investment, it is important to understand the risks associated with Peer-to-Peer lending. Investors should research potential investments and be sure to diversify their investments across a range of loan types in order to minimize risk. By investing in Peer-to-Peer lending, investors can benefit from an attractive return on investment as well as enjoy a sense of satisfaction knowing that they are helping others to access the capital they need. Peer-to-Peer lending can be a great way to make money while making a positive difference in the world at the same time.

The Disadvantage Of Peer-To-Peer Lending As Passive Income

Peer-to-peer lending, while providing individuals with the opportunity to earn passive income, also has its potential downsides. Peer-to-peer lenders bear the credit risk associated with their investments; if a borrower fails to repay their loan, the lender will not receive any return on that investment. Additionally, most platforms charge a service fee for their services, which can reduce the amount of income earned through Peer-to-peer lending. Furthermore, Peer-to-peer lenders must remain aware of all local regulations in relation to Peer-to-peer lending and may face difficulty finding borrowers or lenders in certain areas due to the restrictions imposed by these regulations. As a result, Peer-to-peer lending may not be the best option for individuals looking to generate passive income.

It is important to consider both the potential benefits and risks associated with Peer-to-peer lending before deciding whether or not it is the right investment strategy for you. Peer-to-peer lenders must remain aware of all potential risks and should conduct extensive research before committing to any Peer-to-peer lending opportunity. Additionally, Peer-to-peer lenders should be aware of their financial situation and ability to manage the risks associated with Peer-to-peer lending to maximize their potential return on investment. By considering all of these factors, Peer-to-peer lenders can ensure that Peer-to-peer lending is a viable opportunity for passive income and maximize their potential earnings.

In conclusion, Peer-to-peer lending has the potential to generate passive income for individuals, but it also carries certain risks and requires research and financial management skills in order to be successful. Therefore, peer-to-peer lenders should be aware of all potential risks and benefits associated with Peer-to-peer lending before making any decisions in order to ensure that Peer-to-peer lending is the right fit for them. By doing this, Peer-to-peer lenders can take advantage of the opportunity to generate passive income through Peer-to-peer lending while minimizing their potential risks.

Create A Print-On-Demand Store

Create a print-on-demand store to produce and deliver custom products to customers with minimal effort. With print-on-demand technology, you can create a store that offers anything from t-shirts and mugs to posters and phone cases. All of these items can be printed on demand, shipped directly to the customer, and sold without ever having to store any inventory. Create an online store that showcases your unique designs, and offer customers the convenience of ordering custom items without ever having to leave their home. Create a store that produces trendy and high-quality products to keep up with customer demand so that you can maximize profits. You can create a successful business without investing in expensive tools or equipment with print-on-demand technology. Instead, start a print-on-demand store and make money from designing products that cater to your target audience. Create a passive income stream with no overhead costs or inventory to manage. Create a print-on-demand store today and start making money tomorrow!

Create an online store selling custom and personalized items that can be printed on demand, shipped directly to the customer, and sold without ever having to store any inventory. Create a store that produces trendy and high-quality products to keep up with customer demand, so you can maximize profits. With print-on-demand technology, start your own successful business without investing in expensive tools or equipment. Create an online shop selling unique designs and offer customers the convenience of ordering custom items without ever having to leave their homes.

What Are The Steps For Starting To Create A Print-On-Demand Store?

Starting a print-on-demand store requires a few simple steps. First, you need to decide what kind of products you want to offer. For example, you could create custom t-shirts, mugs, phone cases, or any other product that can be printed on demand. Then, select a printing partner who can help you fulfil orders and print your products. Finally, set up an online store and start marketing your store to potential customers. Using a print-on-demand model, you can generate passive income without worrying about manufacturing or inventory costs. With the right strategies in place, Creating a print-on-demand store could be a great way to make some extra money.

Advantages Of Creating A Print-On-Demand Store

Creating a print-on-demand store is an excellent way to make money passively without having to invest heavily in inventory upfront. You can create designs for t-shirts, mugs, accessories and more and sell them through your store without ever having to worry about stocking or shipping products. Additionally, you will only have to pay for the items once they have already sold, meaning you won't be stuck with unsold inventory. Furthermore, Print-on-demand stores are easy to set up and manage, making them an ideal option for beginners looking to break into e-commerce without having to invest a lot of time and money. Lastly, it's also a great way to test out product ideas and give customers a chance to customize items, which can help you better understand your target audience.

The Disadvantage Of Creating A Print-On-Demand Store

Apart from the advantages, Creating a print-on-demand store also has some disadvantages. One of them is the upfront cost. You may need to pay for the initial setup and inventory costs before you can start selling your products. Moreover, you will incur additional costs in terms of advertising and marketing. Additionally, since it takes time and effort to design and produce custom products, you may need to outsource the task to a third party which can be expensive.

Finally, Creating a print-on-demand store often has lower profit margins compared to traditional retail stores. This is due to the fact that you are selling individual items instead of buying in bulk. Therefore, it is important to be mindful of your costs and choose the right prices for your products.

The Tips For Creating A Print-On-Demand Store

as a passive income idea

1. Create a Unique Brand: Create an identity for your store that stands out from the competition. This can include designing your own logo, colours and fonts, as well as deciding upon themes or product types to specialize in.

2. Find Your Niche: Deciding on a niche will help you to create a loyal customer base and attract buyers who are looking for specific products. This can include focusing on a certain type of product, such as apparel, home decor, artwork, or accessories.

3. Research Your Suppliers: It is important to research the quality and reliability of your suppliers before partnering with them. Look into their reviews, references, and customer satisfaction ratings before selecting a partner.

4. Create Your Store: Many platforms, such as Shopify or Etsy, allow you to create your own store with minimal setup costs and fees. Here, you can customize your store's layout, design, products available, shipping options, payment methods and

more.

5. Promote Your Store: Create an effective digital marketing strategy to get the word out about your store. Consider advertising on social media, creating a blog or website, and leveraging influencers to help spread the word. Additionally, use email campaigns or newsletters to stay in contact with customers and let them know of any new products or deals available.

6. Create Quality Products: Create high-quality products that satisfy customers and ensure they return for more. Offer different designs and options to choose from, as well as gift cards or discounts for repeat purchases.

7. Monitor Your Progress: Track your store's progress and analyze the customer feedback you receive in order to make necessary improvements. Create surveys, review customer service interactions, and look into the user experience on your website to uncover any areas of improvement.

In conclusion, Creating a print-on-demand store is an excellent option if you want to generate passive income innovatively, but it has its own set of challenges. You will need to weigh up both the advantages and disadvantages before taking the plunge.

CHAPER 4 :AFFILIATE MARKETING

A ffiliate marketing is an online marketing strategy in which a business rewards its affiliates for each successful sale made through their referral link. Affiliates can be anyone who promotes the business's product or services, such as bloggers, digital marketers, or influencers. Affiliates are given a unique link containing a tracking code so the business can track and measure their performance. Affiliates earn a commission for each sale generated through their link, and the amount of commission can vary depending on the product or service type. Affiliate marketing is a great way for businesses to gain visibility, increase sales, and build relationships with their affiliates. Affiliate marketing can be incredibly successful, but selecting the right partners and creating a strong marketing strategy is important to ensure maximum success. Affiliate marketing can be an incredibly effective way for businesses to grow and generate revenue, so it is important to understand the basics of affiliate marketing before getting started.

Affiliate programs can be a great way to generate additional income and increase brand recognition, but it is important to understand the fundamentals of affiliate marketing before jumping in. Affiliates need to research potential partners, create a plan for promoting their products or services, and build relationships with their affiliates. Affiliates also need to track and monitor their performance in order to determine which strategies are working best and where they can improve. Affiliate marketing is a powerful tool that can help businesses grow, but it is important to understand the basics before getting started. With proper planning and dedication, affiliate marketing can be an incredibly successful way for businesses to generate additional revenue.

What Are The Steps For Starting An Affiliate Marketing

1. Research Affiliate Programs: Before you begin promoting products and services, it's important to research the different Affiliate programs available so that you can find one that best suits your needs. Consider what types of products or services you would like to promote and make sure the program offers them.

2. Create Your Website or Blog: Affiliate marketing requires having an online presence, such as a website or blog. You will need to create a platform where potential customers can find you, learn about your services and products, and make purchases.

3. Choose Affiliate Products: Once you have created your website or blog, choosing which Affiliate products you would like to promote is time. Affiliate programs offer a variety of different products and services, so be sure to select ones that are relevant to your niche.

4. Sign Up As An Affiliate: After you have chosen the Affiliate products you wish to promote, it is time to sign up as an Affiliate for each program. Affiliate programs will often have an application process and provide Affiliates with

unique tracking codes or links, which you must use to promote their products.

5. Promote Your Affiliate Products: Once you have been accepted as an Affiliate for a particular program, it is time to start promoting their products and services. This can include creating content on your website or blog, writing product reviews, and setting up social media accounts to reach more potential customers.

6. Monitor Affiliate Performance: Regularly monitor the performance of your Affiliate campaigns to ensure that they are performing as expected. This can include tracking clicks, sales, and other key metrics so that you can make changes when needed. Additionally, Affiliate programs often provide Affiliates with detailed reports that contain valuable insights into their performance.

7. Re-Invest Affiliate Earnings: Finally, it is important to re-invest your Affiliate earnings back into your business so that you can continue to grow and reach more potential customers. Affiliate marketing can be a great way to make passive income, but only if you are willing to put in the effort and invest your earnings into furthering your business.

Advantage Of Affiliate Marketing

Affiliate marketing is a great way to increase your online presence and boost revenue. Affiliate programs provide businesses with an excellent opportunity to reach new customers, while also providing affiliates with the chance to earn commissions. Affiliate marketing is advantageous for both sides of the equation, making it one of the most successful forms of digital marketing.

Affiliate programs are highly effective for businesses because they allow them to tap into a vast network of people who are interested in their products or services. Affiliates can help expand their reach and visibility, generate leads, increase sales, and boost brand recognition. Affiliates also benefit from having access to exclusive offers and promotions that may not be available elsewhere. Affiliate marketing is an easy, cost-effective way to leverage the power of online marketing and drive more sales. It's a great way to build customer relationships while also increasing revenue. Affiliate programs are incredibly powerful tools that can help businesses maximize their profits and reach new heights.

The Disadvantages Of Affiliate Marketing

Affiliate Marketing can be a profitable venture, but some potential drawbacks should be taken into consideration. Affiliates may have difficulty generating traffic and converting sales due to competition with other marketers in the same niche. Affiliates may also experience delays in receiving commission payments, as well as long wait times for product delivery or customer service issues. Affiliates may also need to invest in marketing software and tools as well as put time and energy into building relationships with other Affiliate marketers who can provide valuable advice and tips. Finally, Affiliate marketing can be risky if Affiliates don't keep up with changing trends, regulations, and technologies. It is important to stay up to date with the latest Affiliate marketing news and strategies in order to maximize profits. Affiliates should also be aware of potentially fraudulent activities, as these can quickly impact their Affiliate marketing success.

Tips For Affiliate Marketing

1. Choose Affiliate Programs Carefully: Affiliate programs vary in terms of the types of products or services they offer, commission rates, and other factors. Before signing up for any program, take some time to research the various options available and select one that best meets your needs.

2. Promote Quality Content: Affiliate programs become successful when content is shared and promoted in the right places. Quality content should be well-written, relevant to your target

audience, and provide valuable information about the product or service you are promoting.

3. Track Affiliate Performance: Affiliate marketing can generate a lot of income if done correctly, but it's important to track performance on a regular basis. Use software or tools to track the performance of your affiliates and adjust strategies accordingly.

4. Be Engaging: Affiliate marketing success depends on engagement with potential customers. Share content regularly, respond quickly to comments and questions, and interact with affiliates in meaningful ways. This will help keep customers coming back for more.

5. Utilize Affiliate Tracking Tools: Affiliate tracking tools are available to help you track the performance of your affiliates and make sure that payments are being made on time. Use these tools to ensure that everything is running smoothly and all transactions are properly tracked.

6. Monitor Affiliate Spending: Affiliate marketing can be a great source of additional income, but it can also be a drain on your marketing budget if you're not careful. Monitor spending regularly and make sure that resources are being allocated wisely.

7. Diversify Affiliate Programs: Affiliate programs should be diverse to ensure the most success.

Consider using different types of products or services and affiliate programs to ensure that you reach the most potential customers.

8. Leverage Social Media: Affiliate marketing is well-suited for social media promotion since it can be shared easily among friends, family, and followers. Popular platforms like Facebook, Instagram, and more are utilised to reach a wide audience.

9. Promote Affiliates Strategically: Affiliate marketing should be strategically promoted to reach the right people and generate the most income. Utilize advertising and promotional tools like email marketing, banner ads, and more to ensure your content reaches its intended target audience.

10. Offer Affiliates Incentives: Affiliates want to make money, so incentivizing them with bonuses or discounts can help increase sales and drive more traffic. Consider offering incentives like free shipping, product coupons, or other rewards to encourage Affiliates to promote your products.

In conclusion, Affiliate Marketing is an effective way to make money online, but Affiliates must be willing to put in the effort necessary to make a profitable venture. Affiliates should also be aware of potential drawbacks such as competition, delays in payment, marketing tools and fraudulent activity. Affiliate marketers must be prepared to invest time and energy into building their Affiliate network and staying up to date with the latest Affiliate trends.

CHAPER 5 :
SELLING

S ell photography online can be a great way to make money as a creative. It can also provide an opportunity to gain exposure and recognition for your work. There are several ways to sell photography online, including selling prints or products through established platforms such as Etsy or Society6 or offering digital downloads via services like Sellfy. With Sellfy, you can easily create and customize a store to market and sell your photos. Sellfy allows you to accept payments securely and quickly, so you can get paid instantly after each sale. You also have the option of setting up subscription services, allowing customers to purchase access to your photo library on an ongoing basis. Sellfy provides automated marketing tools that help you promote your work to a larger audience. Sellfy makes it easy to start selling photography online and turn your passion into a profitable business.

For those interested in creating their own independent storefront, Sellfy offers advanced customization options so you can create a unique website that reflects your personal style. Sellfy also allows you to manage orders, track customers, and access valuable analytics, giving you complete control over your business. With Sellfy's powerful tools and features, you can easily create and manage a successful online photography business.

What Are The Steps For Starting To Sell Photography Online?

1. Identify your photography niche: Before you begin selling photography online, you must first identify your niche. Consider what type of pictures you want to sell, such as landscapes, portraits, wildlife photographs or fashion images.

2. Develop your brand and website/portfolio: Building a strong personal brand is essential for photographers who wish to sell their work online. This includes having a website or portfolio that showcases your photography in the best light and conveys the type of images you offer.

3. Sell on stock photo websites: Selling photos on stock photo websites is one of the most popular

ways for photographers to make money online. Websites such as Shutterstock, iStock and Adobe allow photographers to upload their photos for sale.

4. Sell through microstock agencies: Microstock photography websites enable photographers to sell their photos royalty-free. They are generally less expensive than stock photo sites but offer a smaller potential return.

5. Sell prints online: Selling prints online is another way to earn money from your photography. You can set up your own e-commerce website to sell prints or use platforms such as Society6, SmugMug and Etsy to host and sell your prints.

6. Sell digital downloads: Digital downloads are a great way for photographers to make money online. Sellers can set up their own websites or use platforms such as Sellfy to offer digital downloads of their photos.

7. Sell physical goods: Selling physical goods such as calendars, mugs and t-shirts featuring photography is another popular way for photographers to make money online. You can create your own store on websites like Shopify or use print-on-demand websites such as Redbubble or Zazzle.

8. Offer tutorials and courses: Sellers can also

make money online by offering photography tutorials, courses and e-books. Platforms such as Teachable and Skillshare enable photographers to set up their own courses and earn a commission on each sale.

9. License your photos: Sellers can also license their photos to companies, publications and other organizations who may wish to use their images in products or publications. Licensing agreements typically involve a one-time payment or recurring fees depending on the terms of the agreement.

10. Network and market yourself: Finally, networking and marketing yourself as a photographer is essential for finding clients and customers. Sellers should use social media platforms, email campaigns and search engine optimization to spread the word about their business. Sellers can also attend photography conventions and market their services in person.

Advantage Of Sell Photography Online

Selling photography online has many advantages. First, photographers can quickly and easily reach a wider audience than ever before. By leveraging the power of the internet, photographs can be bought and sold in a matter of minutes—allowing photographers to make money more quickly and efficiently. Additionally, photography of sale online helps to eliminate some of the barriers to entry for new photographers, such as the cost of traditional printing and gallery fees. With online platforms, photographers have access to a global customer base at a minimal cost.

Furthermore, selling photography online helps to increase the value of individual images by allowing them to be easily shared and distributed. Sellers can quickly reach more customers with digital photos since they do not have to worry about the cost of printing and shipping physical prints. Sellers can also take advantage of digital marketing platforms such as social media and email marketing to reach a wide range of potential customers.

The Disadvantages Of Sell Photography Online

Unfortunately, selling photography online is not without its drawbacks. Sellers must consider the potential of their work being reproduced or stolen, as digital images can be easily shared and distributed without proper permission. There is also the risk that some buyers may fail to pay what they owe for purchased photographs, which could be a considerable financial loss for photographers. Additionally, online sales are subject to marketplace fees, commissions, and applicable taxes. Sellers must also consider the cost of hosting their own website or store and may need to invest in adequate marketing strategies to ensure their work is seen by potential buyers. Finally, there may be legal issues involved with selling photography online; for example, some images may require a copyright license or permission from the subject of the photograph in order to be sold. Sellers should familiarize themselves with local laws and regulations before beginning to sell photographs online.

Tips For Sell Photography Online

Selling photography online is a great way to make money from your artistic talent and skills. However, there are several steps you need to take in order to set up an effective business that will generate consistent income. Here are some tips for selling photography online:

1. Create a Quality Website – The first step in selling photography online is to create a quality website that showcases your portfolio, provides visitors with easy-to-find contact information and clearly outlines your services. It is essential to have a professional, user-friendly website which will allow potential customers to browse your photography portfolios.

2. Develop an Easy Payment System – Sellers

should also invest in a secure payment system that makes it easy for customers to purchase your photography online. Popular payment services include PayPal or Google Checkout, which can be integrated into your website.

3. Offer Special Deals and Promotions – Sellers should also consider offering special discounts and promotions in order to attract more potential customers. This could include introducing loyalty programs that offer discounts after certain purchases or having a one-time special deal that new customers can take advantage of.

4. Use Social Media – Sellers should also make sure they are taking advantage of social media as part of their selling strategy. Platforms such as Instagram, Twitter and Facebook can help spread the word about your business and reach out to more potential customers.

Overall, selling photography online is an excellent way for photographers to expand their customer base, increase their income, and create more opportunities to promote their work. With the right tools and strategies, selling photography online can be a great way for photographers to take their business to the next level.

Sell Digital Products

Sell digital products as a passive income idea is one

of the most popular ways to generate an income stream. There are many advantages to selling digital products, such as low overhead costs, no inventory storage and easy scalability. Plus, you can reach customers all around the world.

If you're creative and tech-savvy, this can be a great way to make money. You can create digital products, like eBooks, online courses, music and films, apps, templates or plugins. Then, sell these through your own website or on popular marketplaces such as Amazon Kindle Store, iTunes and Google Play.

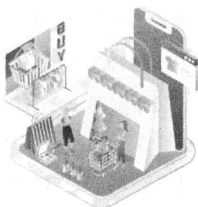

When creating your digital products, you'll need to consider price, quality, content and delivery. In addition, make sure your products are up-to-date and well-presented to ensure they're attractive to customers. You can also offer discounts or bundle deals to encourage people to buy more of your products.

Once you have created the digital products, you need to build an audience for them. Promote your products through SEO, social media or paid advertising campaigns. You should also build an email list to communicate with your customers and let them know of any new products you have released.

What Are The Steps For Starting Selling Digital Products?

1. Identify what digital products you want to sell. Examples of digital products include eBooks, membership sites, online courses, video series and software applications. Consider creating something new that hasn't been done before or selling existing popular products that have already proven successful.

2. Figure out how you plan to deliver your digital products. You can create a digital delivery system or use an online platform such as Shopify or Sellfy, which provide convenient options to store and sell digital products from a secure website.

3. Create marketing materials for your digital product. Generate interest by creating promotional videos, writing blog posts, engaging on social media and offering discounts.

4. Develop a pricing strategy that will maximize your profits while still being competitive in the marketplace.

5. Create an effective sales funnel to convert leads into buyers and drive repeat purchases. Offer free trial downloads, promote bundles and include upsells at checkout to boost revenue.

6. Set up payment processing for your digital products. For example, you can use a payment gateway such as PayPal or Stripe, which makes it easy to accept payments online.

7. Promote your digital product by advertising on popular websites and getting influencers to review and recommend it. Leverage the power of email marketing to nurture leads and drive sales.

8. Monitor your sales and analytics to measure the success of your digital product. Then, make changes where needed and continue refining your marketing strategy to maximize profits.

Advantage Of Selling Digital Products

Selling digital products as a passive income can be extremely lucrative and is an attractive way to make money without actively working. Digital products such as ebooks, courses, music, software, design elements and more can be sold online to generate a long-term income. With digital products, there's no need for physical inventory or shipping costs, meaning you can make a much higher profit per item sold. Additionally, once digital products are created, you can sell them multiple times without any additional effort. You also have the opportunity to reach a global audience, as digital products can be sold to anyone with an internet connection. This is a great way to expand your reach and increase your earning potential.

Furthermore, digital products offer you the opportunity to build up a loyal customer base with repeat buyers who return for more of your content. Finally, selling digital products online requires minimal overhead and effort – making it an ideal choice for passive income. So sell digital products today and start making money without actively working!

All these advantages make selling digital products an attractive passive income idea that should be seriously considered. With minimal effort, you can easily create a long-term stream of income that will provide you with financial security for years to come.

The Disadvantage Of Selling Digital Products

One disadvantage of selling digital products as a passive income idea is that you must have the skills and abilities to create quality digital products. It can be difficult to ensure your product stands out from the rest or meets customer expectations. Additionally, finding the right customers for your product requires marketing savvy and knowledge on pricing and promotion. Finally, you will need to be comfortable with technology in order to create digital products that are user-friendly and secure. All of this can take a significant amount of time and effort before you start to see the results of your efforts.

Another disadvantage is that digital product sales can be very competitive, especially if there are already established digital products out there in the same field. Therefore, you will have to be creative and find ways to differentiate your product from the competition. Additionally, you will need to develop an effective marketing plan that can help you reach potential customers and build a loyal customer base. All of this takes careful planning and dedication, which may prove difficult for those who are inexperienced in this field.

Finally, you will need to be comfortable with digital payment systems and other methods for securely storing customer data. This complex undertaking could take more time than expected if you don't have the necessary expertise. Additionally, the lack of physical contact with customers may make it difficult to build relationships with them and increase customer loyalty.

Tips For Sell Digital Products

1. Choose the right products to sell - It is important to choose digital products that are attractive and valuable to your target audience. First, do some

research to find out what they are looking for, and then create or source products that meet their needs.

2. Create marketing materials - Good digital products need good marketing. So create attractive and informative product pages, write compelling descriptions, and develop promotional materials such as email newsletters, webinars, and videos.

3. Utilize social media - Reach out to potential customers through popular social media platforms like Facebook and Twitter. Use these platforms for advertising your products, engaging with potential customers, and building loyal followers.

4. Sell through an online marketplace - Sell your products through an established online marketplace such as Amazon or eBay. This will give you access to a larger potential customer base, as well as tools to manage inventory and process payments.

5. Investigate automation - Automation can help you maximize the potential of your digital products. Investigate solutions such as software bots, virtual assistants, and other technologies that can help you sell more efficiently.

6. Make customer service a priority - Good customer service is essential for any business, and it is especially important when you are selling

digital products. Build systems to handle inquiries and complaints quickly and efficiently, and strive to provide an excellent customer experience.

7. Measure your success - Track the performance of your digital products and look for areas to improve. Use data to refine your product offerings, create better marketing materials, and find new ways to reach customers. This will help you maximize the success of your digital products over time.

By following these tips, you can increase the success of selling digital products as a passive income source. Whether you are just getting started or have been in the industry for years, these tips will help you make the most of your digital products.

Sell Handmade Goods

Sell handmade goods as a passive income idea by creating products that people will love. You can create anything from jewelry to pottery, clothing or even home decor items. Sell your handmade goods on websites such as Etsy and eBay, or you could even open up your own online store. You can also sell at local craft fairs and markets to reach an even wider audience. With this passive income idea, you can use your creativity and artistic talents to make money without investing a lot of time or money.

You could also consider partnering with local businesses that are looking for unique products to offer their customers. This allows you to expand your customer reach and increase your potential for sales. You could also consider setting up a subscription service where customers can sign up to receive unique handmade products on a monthly basis. This would provide you with a consistent source of passive income that doesn't require you to constantly work on creating new items.

What Are The Steps For Starting Sell Handmade Goods As A Passive Income?

1. Identify what handmade goods you want to sell: The first step in starting a successful passive income business selling handmade goods is to identify the type of product you want to sell. Consider factors such as your interests, skills, and the current market demand when selecting your

product.

2. Research the market: Once you have identified the handmade goods you want to sell, it is important to do some research into the current market for that product. Check out popular online stores, craft markets and other handmade goods sellers to understand pricing, trends, and what type of customers are interested in your product.

3. Set up a website: Setting up a website is essential for selling handmade goods online as it gives you a platform to showcase your products and engage with potential customers. Consider using an e-commerce platform such as Shopify or BigCommerce to set up your store quickly and easily.

4. Source materials: Before you can start selling your handmade goods, you need to source the necessary materials. Research suppliers and decide where you will purchase your materials, considering the price, quality and sustainability.

5. Design and create: Now you have sourced the materials, it is time to design and create your handmade goods. Utilize your skills and creativity to produce attractive and high-quality products that your customers will love.

6. Launch and Sell: Once you have created a few products, it is time to launch your store and start selling! Use online marketing techniques such as

SEO, PPC, content creation and social media to reach potential customers. Additionally, consider setting up a presence at local craft markets and events.

Advantage Of Selling Handmade Goods

a passive income idea is that you can create and make items in your spare time and then sell them online or through a local craft market. You can choose the types of items you want to make and the materials you'd like to use, allowing for personal creativity and passion. You don't need to deeply understand business to get started, as many resources are available on the internet to guide you. Selling handmade goods allows for flexible scheduling and working from home if needed. You can also use it an opportunity to network with other experienced crafters or entrepreneurs in the same field.

The Disadvantage Of Selling Handmade Goods

One of the biggest disadvantages of selling handmade goods as a passive income idea is the amount of time and effort it takes to create them. While you can make some money from your products, it won't be an immediate or fast-paced return like investing in stocks or real estate. Design, create, and market the product often requires days, weeks, or even months. Additionally, it can be difficult to find a dedicated customer base or build brand recognition with handmade goods. Finally, competition from other artists in the same space can make it tough for your products to stand out. All of these issues mean that you may not see a return on your investment as quickly as you would with other forms of passive income.

Tips For Selling Handmade Goods

1. Find your niche: Sell handmade products that are in demand and unique. Focus on what you know best and specialize in a product or set of products that set you apart from the competition.

2. Utilize online platforms: Take advantage of popular online marketplaces such as Etsy, eBay, or Amazon to reach a wider audience. Sell your handmade goods on social media sites like Instagram, Twitter, and Facebook to engage with potential customers.

3. Set competitive prices: Research the market and set prices that are fair and reasonable so that your products remain competitive in the marketplace.

4. Promote your product: Create promotions and incentives to draw attention to your products. Leverage influencers and other forms of digital

marketing to reach new customers.

5. Focus on quality: Ensure that you are producing high-quality products that will keep customers coming back for more. Invest in quality materials, craftsmanship, and customer service to ensure a positive experience for every buyer.

6. Track your progress: Pay attention to the data and analytics associated with your product sales. Monitor trending topics, customer reviews, and other feedback to help drive improvements in your products and business.

However, if you're willing to put in the effort and have a unique product that differentiates itself from competitors, selling handmade goods can be a viable source of income. Additionally, it can be very rewarding to share your art and bring joy to customers who appreciate your hard work. Therefore, with the right strategy, you can use Selling handmade goods as an effective passive income stream.

Overall, Selling handmade goods is a great way to make money passively, but it requires time and effort upfront to create the product and build a customer base. It may not be the fastest or most reliable source of income, but with patience and dedication, it can be a very rewarding venture.

CHAPER 6 : AN E-COMMERCE BUSINESS

Start an e-commerce business to build a passive income stream. With the rise of technology, it's never been easier to set up and manage an e-commerce store on your own. All you need is a computer, internet access, and the right resources to get started.

The first step in starting an e-commerce business is to figure out what kind of products you want to sell. After that, you can either source products from wholesalers and distributors or create your own unique products, depending on the type of business model that you're going for.

Once you've decided on a product range, creating your online store is next. To do this, you'll need an e-commerce platform such as Shopify, Magento, or WooCommerce. These platforms provide you with an easy-to-use interface to manage your store and process orders.

What Are The Steps For Starting An E-Commerce Business?

Starting an e-commerce business can seem intimidating, but it is possible to make a passive income with the right guidance. Here are the steps you should take when starting your own e-commerce business:

1. Research – Start by researching the industry, your competitors, and potential markets to target. You will also want to determine what type of products you want to sell and how they will be delivered.

2. Develop your Business Plan – Start by creating a detailed business plan outlining goals, objectives, strategies, target market and estimated costs. Ensure that the plan is comprehensive and answers any questions about the direction of your e-commerce business.

3. Choose a business structure – Choose the legal entity that best suits your business. Options include sole proprietorships, partnerships, LLCs and corporations.

4. Obtain Required Licenses & permits – Research what licenses and permits are required in your area for an e-commerce business to operate legally.

5. Set up Your E-commerce Platform – A platform is needed to display and manage your products, take payments and handle customer service. Popular options include Shopify, Amazon, eBay, Bigcommerce, Volusion and Magento.

6. Start Marketing Your Business – Start marketing your business through search engine optimization (SEO) campaigns, social media ads and email campaigns to reach potential customers.

7. Launch Your Business – Start selling your products and services online, and make sure to stay on top of customer service inquiries and order fulfillment.

Advantage Start An E-Commerce Business

Start an e-commerce business as a passive income and you will be able to make money while you sleep. With the right strategy and tools, you can create an online store that will generate revenue with minimal effort. An e-commerce business is relatively easy to set up and maintain, and it allows you to reach a much larger audience than any traditional brick-and-mortar store. Plus, you can use digital marketing techniques that make it easier than ever to connect with potential customers and increase your sales.

You don't need a lot of capital to get started – all you really need is the right tools and technology, plus a little bit of knowledge on how to create an online store that will bring in customers effectively. With the right combination of products, services, and marketing tactics, you can build an e-commerce business that will generate recurring income for years to come.

Once your store is up and running, it's important to stay on top of trends in the industry and use analytics to track your progress. You can also take advantage of automation tools that enable you to manage your store with minimal effort. With these strategies and the right attitude, you can grow an e-commerce business that will provide a steady source of passive income. So start today and soon, you'll be reaping the rewards of this lucrative venture!

Disadvantage Starting An E-Commerce Business

can be a great way to make passive income, but it's not for everyone. Before jumping into the world of e-commerce, it's important to weigh some potential drawbacks of starting an online business.

One potential downside is the cost associated with setting up and running an e-commerce business. Start-up costs can include website hosting, shopping cart software, marketing costs and more. Additionally, many e-commerce businesses require significant time to run and maintain. This could mean long hours of research, customer service and product development that may not be feasible if you already have a full-time job or other commitments.

Another potential downside is the competition. Again, it can be difficult to stand out in a crowded e-commerce space, and you may find yourself competing with larger, more established companies that have lower prices or better customer service. But, again, if you lack the necessary skills or experience, it may be difficult to navigate this competitive environment.

Finally, there is the risk of failure. Starting an e-commerce business can be risky, and there is no guarantee of success. You may find that you have to make substantial investments in your business before seeing any returns, and even then, there is no guarantee that the business will be profitable.

Before embarking on an e-commerce venture, it's important to consider all of these potential disadvantages. While starting an e-commerce business can be a great source of passive income, there are risks and challenges associated with the process that must be taken into account.

Tips For Starting An E-Commerce Business

Starting an e-commerce business can be a great way to generate a passive income stream for yourself. However, it can be overwhelming the first time you dive in. Here are some tips that will help you get started:

1. Start small and don't try to do too much at once. Start with one product or service and build from there. Start with a basic website design and add features as needed.

2. Research the competition. Find out what competitors in your niche are doing and how they're reaching customers. Knowing this information can help you create an effective marketing plan for your own business.

3. Consider dropshipping. If you don't want to handle the shipping process yourself, dropshipping can be a great way to outsource the task. You'll have more time to work on other aspects of your business while someone else fulfils orders.

4. Invest in marketing and promotion. Once your website is up and running, make sure people know about it. Start building a presence on social media and invest in advertising if possible.

5. Be patient and stay focused. Starting an e-commerce business isn't something you can do overnight — it will take time, effort, and patience to see results. So keep your focus on the long-term goals of your business for the best results.

Starting an e-commerce business can be a great way to make passive income, but it's important to do your research and take the time to develop a plan before you get started.

Dividend Stocks

Dividend stocks are a popular investment option for those seeking to build wealth over time. Dividends are regular payments companies make to their shareholders, usually quarterly or annually. Dividend stocks have the potential to provide investors with a steady income from their investments as well as capital appreciation when the stock's price increases. Dividend stocks can be a great addition to a portfolio, as they can provide investors with a steady income stream. Dividend stocks also offer investors the potential for capital gains when stock prices increase in value. Dividend stocks tend to be more stable than other investments and have lower risk levels than other types of investments. Dividend stocks are attractive for those looking for long-term investments that provide a steady income. Dividend stocks are also attractive for those looking to diversify their portfolio, as they can often offer a hedge against market volatility. Dividend stocks can be an excellent investment option for those seeking to generate long-term wealth and income. For investors looking to build wealth over time, dividend stocks can be a smart way to do so. Dividend stocks offer investors the potential for both income and capital gains over time, making them an excellent choice for diversifying their portfolios and generating long-term returns. Dividend stocks can also be used as part of a strategy to hedge against market volatility and reduce risk levels.

What are the steps for starting Dividend stocks?

1. Establish an Investment Goal: It is important to have a clear investment goal when considering Dividend stocks. Diversifying your portfolio with Dividend stocks can help you achieve different

goals, including income generation, capital appreciation and stability.

2. Do Your Research: Dividend stock investments involve researching the company's financial standing and historical performance to determine its growth potential. Researching potential Dividend stocks will help you make informed investment decisions and better understand the risk associated with each company.

3. Choose Dividend Stocks: Once you have identified your investment goal, researched Dividend stocks and determined which ones best fit your objective, you can start investing. Dividend stocks are available through online brokers or mutual funds that specialize in Dividend investing.

4. Monitor Your Dividend Stocks: It is important to monitor your Dividend stocks and stay informed on any news that could impact their performance. You should also regularly review the financial statements of Dividend stocks to ensure that they are still meeting your investment goals.

5. Diversify: Diversifying your Dividend stock investments can help you spread the risk across different sectors and industries and enhance returns by taking advantage of multiple opportunities. Investing in various Dividend stocks with varying dividend yields, payout ratios and other factors can help you reduce risk and

maximize returns.

By following these steps, Dividend stock investors can build a portfolio of Dividend stocks that meet their investment objectives and provide them with a steady income and potential capital growth. As a result, dividend stocks can be an attractive option for long-term investments.

Advantages of Dividend stocks

Dividend stocks offer a variety of advantages to investors. Dividend stocks provide a steady source of income, as companies typically pay out dividends at regular intervals. Dividends are usually paid out in cash, which can be used to increase your portfolio's liquidity or reinvested into additional dividend-paying stocks. Dividends also tend to be more resilient during tough economic times and stock market downturns, offering protection when other investments may falter.

Dividend stocks are also beneficial for those who are looking for long-term income or retirement income, as dividends can provide a steady stream of income for years to come. Dividend stocks can also serve as a hedge against inflation, as the income from

dividend payments typically increases over time. Dividend stocks also have the potential for capital appreciation when the stock price rises. Finally, dividend stocks can be a good way to diversify an investment portfolio and help spread out risk. Dividends provide a steady source of income that can help protect against downturns in other investments.

By incorporating dividend stocks into an investment portfolio, investors can benefit from the steady income stream, diversification of risk, and potential for capital appreciation. Dividend stocks are an important part of an investor's portfolio, as they offer a range of advantages that can help achieve financial goals. Dividend stocks should be selected carefully and monitored periodically to meet the investor's needs.

the disadvantages of dividend stocks

Dividend stocks are a great way to earn income from your investments, but investing in them has some drawbacks. Dividends can be unreliable since companies might choose to reduce or eliminate them at any time. Dividend stocks are also less attractive in times of economic downturns, as companies may reduce or suspend their dividends due to a lack of profits. Dividend stocks are also more volatile than other types of investments, as the stock market can quickly change and cause prices to fluctuate significantly. Finally, dividend stocks tend to have higher taxes on their income since they are considered taxable. These drawbacks can be difficult to manage, so it is important to understand the risks associated with dividend stocks before investing in them.

Tips For Dividend Stocks

1. Do your research: Dividend stocks may look attractive in the short term, but it's important to do your homework before making an investment. For example, look into a company's past performance, financial statements and dividend history to confirm that it is a good long-term investment choice.

2. Diversify: Diversifying your portfolio is always good when investing in dividend stocks. Dividend-paying stocks can come from many different industries and sectors, so it's important to spread out your investments to lower the risk of any one stock performing poorly.

3. Pay attention to taxation: Dividends may be subject to taxes, so it's important to understand the tax implications of investing in dividend stocks. Dividends can be taxed at different rates depending on the type of stock and how long you have owned it, so make sure you're aware of this prior to investing.

4. Consider reinvestment: Dividend reinvestment

plans (DRIPs) are available for most dividend-paying stocks and can help to maximize your total returns over the long term. Dividend reinvestment plans allow you to automatically reinvest your dividends in additional shares of the same stock, which can result in larger gains over time.

5. Monitor your investments: Dividends may change periodically, so it's important to stay up-to-date on any changes in dividend payments. In addition, dividend stocks should be monitored regularly to ensure the company is still performing well and the dividends are still being paid out. If anything changes, you may need to reconsider your investment strategy.

Dividend stocks can be a great way to earn income from your investments if you are willing to accept the risks and potential drawbacks. Dividend stocks tend to have higher taxes and can be more volatile than other types of investments. They can also be unreliable in times of economic downturns. Therefore, it is important to understand the risks associated with dividend stocks.

When deciding whether or not to invest in Dividend stocks, it is important to fully understand the risks associated with them and weigh the potential for returns against these risks. Dividend stocks can be a great way to earn income from investments, but it is also important to remember that there are potential drawbacks.

By taking the time to understand Dividend stocks and their associated risks, you can make an informed decision about whether or not Dividend stocks are right for you. If you decide that Dividend stocks are the right investment for you, make sure to do your research and be as informed as possible about the risks associated with Dividend stocks before investing in them.

Start A Dropshipping Store

Start a dropshipping store and enjoy the freedom of passive income. With a dropshipping store, you are maintaining any inventory or handling to maintain any inventory or handle customer orders yourself. All you need is a website and a reliable supplier to fulfill your orders for you. You simply list products from your supplier on your site, and when customers purchase them, you forward their order on to the supplier who ships them directly to your customer. You get paid a profit on each sale with no need for any upfront cost or risk. Start a dropshipping store today and generate passive income from anywhere in the world!

With drop shipping, you can set up an online

store without worrying about inventory, storage costs, and shipping. You can choose to work with a supplier that offers dropshipping services, or you can purchase products in bulk and then ship them out yourself. Once you source your products, all you need is a website and an online payment processor to start selling. All payments will be directly deposited into your bank account, making it easy for you to track your income and profits – a great way to start earning passive income.

What Are The Steps For Starting Start A Dropshipping Store?

Starting a dropshipping store is an excellent passive income opportunity. It requires minimal upfront investment, and you can get started quickly with few technical skills. Here are the steps to start your own store:

1. Choose a Niche – Start by deciding on the type of products you would like to sell in your store. Consider researching popular trends and products in your desired niche, as well as the competition.

2. Research Suppliers – Once you have chosen the type of products you want to sell, Start researching potential suppliers for those items. Look at pricing, shipping times, quality of product, and customer service. You should also find out if there are any dropshipping fees associated with

the supplier.

3. Build Your Store – You will need to choose an e-commerce platform, such as Shopify or WooCommerce, and create your store. This may involve setting up payment systems, designing a website layout, adding product descriptions and images, etc.

4. Start Marketing – Start advertising and marketing your store. This could include content creation, SEO (search engine optimization), social media marketing, PPC (pay-per-click) ads, email campaigns, etc.

5. Monitor Performance – Start tracking your store's performance by monitoring sales figures and customer feedback. Make adjustments to your advertising and marketing strategies if necessary.

Advantage Of Starting A Dropshipping Store

One of the major advantages of starting a dropshipping store is that it can be done with minimal upfront capital. Since you don't have to purchase and hold any inventory, there's no need to order large tities or store products in your own warehouse. This makes it possible for anyone with an internet connection and a few hundred dollars in start-up funds to start a dropshipping store.

Another great advantage of starting a dropshipping store is the low overhead associated with the business. With no inventory to maintain, you don't have to worry about stocking products or managing storage space. This makes it easy to keep your costs low while still providing customers with quality goods and services.

Additionally, starting a dropshipping store is relatively easy to do. With the help of e-commerce platforms like Shopify, WooCommerce and Bigcommerce, setting up an online store has never been easier. All you have to do is choose a platform and design your storefront, upload your products and set up shipping options for customers.

Finally, starting a dropshipping store can be an incredibly rewarding experience. You have the freedom to create your own online business and determine your own success. You'll also be able to build relationships with suppliers and customers over time, which can help you grow your business even more.

The Disadvantages Of Starting A Dropshipping Store

is that it can be difficult to source reliable suppliers and products, as well as to manage customer service and fulfillment. Furthermore, dropshipping requires a significant amount of time and effort in order to research the right suppliers and products, develop an effective marketing plan, keep up with trends in the industry, track inventory levels, etc. Additionally, profit margins are often slim, which means that it may be difficult to generate a significant amount of revenue. Finally, Start a dropshipping store is subject to the same risks as any other online business, such as hacking and fraud. For these reasons, Start a dropshipping store requires careful consideration before investing money or time into it. While Start a dropshipping store can be a great passive income idea, the risks should not be taken lightly. Ultimately Start a dropshipping store requires research, planning, and dedication to ensure success.

The Tips For Starting A Dropshipping Store

Starting a dropshipping store can be an incredibly rewarding experience, especially when done correctly. Here are some tips on how to get started:

1. Start with research: Before jumping into the world of dropshipping, it's important to do your due diligence and thoroughly research the business model. Look at industry trends, competitor models, target market and audience,

and analyze what's working and what isn't.

2. Choose a niche: Once you've done your research, it's time to decide on a niche or specific product line for your dropshipping store. Selecting the right niche can be one of your most critical decisions. It's important to consider what products you can offer that stand out from your competitors.

3. Obtain the necessary licenses: Once you have chosen a niche and a product line, it's essential to obtain the proper licenses to do business in your area. This often includes an e-commerce license as well as any other applicable permits.

4. Find a reliable dropshipping partner: Start by researching contact information for several potential vendors and inquire about their terms and conditions. This is an important step as it can affect your ability to make money over the long-term. It's essential to have clear policies in place regarding returns, shipping times, and product quality.

5. Start marketing: Start by creating an online presence for your business and establish a regular, consistent marketing campaign. This could include content marketing, email campaigns, social media outreach, or even paid advertisements.

Following these steps can help you get started

with your own dropshipping store and generate a passive income. Start by doing research, choosing a niche, obtaining the necessary licenses, finding a reliable partner, and starting marketing. With some dedication and hard work you'll soon be able to reap the rewards of your own dropshipping store.

CHAPER 7 :
RENTING

R ental income

Rental income is income that is earned by renting out a property or space. Rental income typically comes from tenants paying rent on an apartment, house, commercial space, or other real estate properties. Rental income can be an important source of passive income for landlords and investors who can capitalise off the potential in their rental units. Rental income has the potential to increase significantly with proper management and upkeep of the property. Rental income is still subject to taxation, however, landlords may be able to deduct expenses associated with the rental property from their taxable income. Rental income can provide a steady source of passive income and can be used by landlords as a way to supplement their primary sources of income. Rental income can also be used to cover mortgage payments and other expenses. Rental income can be a great way for landlords to maximize their return on investment in rental properties while also providing an important service to tenants.

Renting out property is not without its risks, however. Landlords are responsible for ensuring that their rental units meet safety standards and comply with local codes and regulations. Landlords are also responsible for collecting rent from tenants, maintaining the property, and responding to tenant complaints. Rental income can provide a great source of passive income, but landlords need to be aware that they will also face potential risks.

Rental income can be an important source of passive income, but it should not be taken lightly. Before investing in rental property, landlords should research to ensure they understand the local rules and regulations, potential risks, and the income potential of the rental units they are considering. Rental income can be a great way to generate passive income, but good planning and proper management are key to ensuring that the rental units are successful.

What Are The Steps For Starting Rental Income?

Starting a rental income business requires careful planning and execution. The first step is identifying the type of property you want to rent out and the target market you want to serve. You should also consider the location and cost of acquiring your rental property, as well as any potential expenses associated with running the business.

Once you have determined the rental property and target market, it is important to create a realistic budget based on your expected income and expenses. You should also consider factors such as insurance costs, maintenance and repair costs, and any other associated rental expenses.

After determining the budget, you should research the local rental laws and regulations to ensure that your business complies with all applicable rules. This is important for both landlords and tenants. You should also talk to an accountant or tax advisor about the rules and regulations associated with rental income.

It is also important to research the local real estate market and understand what types of rental properties are in demand. This will help you decide on a reasonable rate to charge as well as the most effective way to market and advertise your rental property.

Finally, you should make sure to screen tenants carefully and set up a clear rental agreement. This will help to ensure that your tenants are responsible and respectful of the property, as well as protect you from potential legal issues.

Starting a rental income business can be both rewarding and profitable, but it requires careful planning and research. By understanding the local laws and regulations, creating a realistic budget, and screening tenants carefully, you can ensure the success of your rental income business.

Advantage Of Rental Income

One of the biggest advantages of rental income is that it can be highly reliable and predictable. Rental income typically follows a fixed monthly schedule, making it easy to budget for and plan for the future. Rental income is also usually consistent over time as long as vacancies are few and far between. Rental income also generally increases over time as rents rise along with inflation and the cost of living. Rental income also offers tax advantages for landlords. Rental income can be depreciated, allowing owners to reduce their taxable income from rental operations while still being able to benefit from the long-term appreciation of property values in many cases.

Rental income is also attractive to investors because it can provide a source of passive income that does not require much ongoing effort or involvement. Rental income can also be used to leverage other investments, such as stocks and bonds, since the cash flow from rental properties provides extra funds for diversification purposes. Finally, rental income offers stability in times of economic uncertainty, since it can continue to flow in even when other investments may not. Rental income can be a great way to generate long-term, reliable income and can provide a boost to your overall financial portfolio.

The Disadvantages Of Rental Income

Rental income can be unpredictable and unreliable. Lords often experience months of no rent payments or tenants not paying their full due amount. Rental income is often dependent on the market and economic conditions. There can be periods of time when people choose to rent instead of buy, or vice versa, affecting the amount of money a landlord can make. Rental income also requires landlords to take on certain responsibilities, such as taking care of repairs and maintenance, collecting rent payments, and dealing with tenants. It can be a time-consuming endeavour that requires landlords to have the right skill set to manage it. Finally, rental income can be subject to taxes, reducing the amount of money landlords earn. Rental income may not be the best option for someone who is looking for reliable and consistent income. However, it can be a great source of supplemental income for those who are willing to take on the responsibilities and risks that come with it. Rental income can also be very profitable, depending on the market conditions and the time and effort spent managing it. Ultimately, rental income can be a great option for those who are willing to take on the risks and responsibilities associated with it. With the right amount of dedication, rental income can be a great source of supplemental or even primary income.

Rent Out A Parking Space

With the rise of ride-sharing services, many people choose to not own a car and rely on these for their transportation needs. Many of them have an extra parking space that can be rented out to those who need it. Renting out your parking space can provide you with additional income while helping meet the parking needs of others.

When you decide to rent out your space, it's important to be aware of local laws and regulations governing renting out a parking space. You will also want to consider what type of agreement you want with the renter, such as if you require a deposit or how long the renter is allowed to stay. Additionally, you'll need to decide if you want your renters to register their vehicles with the city or state and what other rules they must adhere to while using your space.

What Are The Steps For Starting Rent Out A Parking Space?

1. Determine the legal requirements to rent out a parking space. Depending on where you live, different laws and regulations may apply that may affect your ability to rent out a parking space. Therefore, it is important to research the laws and regulations in your area before proceeding any further with this process.

2. Evaluate the layout of your parking space and its location. You will need to consider the size of the parking space, access points, visibility from the nearby street, and any other factors that may affect someone's decision to rent it out.

3. Set a Rent Amount for the Space: Determine how much you would like to charge for renting out your parking space. You should research what other people in your area are charging for similar parking spots so you can set a competitive price.

4. Advertise the Rent Space: Once you have an idea

of how much to charge, you will need to advertise the rent space. Consider using online websites or apps dedicated to connecting people looking to rent parking spots with people who are looking to rent out their spaces. You may also choose to post flyers in your neighbourhood or advertise on local radio stations or newspapers.

5. Draft a Rent Agreement: It is important to draw up a rental agreement that outlines the terms and conditions of renting out the space as well as any additional requirements, such as parking hours or access to the space.

6. Collect Rent: Once you find a renter, you should collect an initial payment upfront and then set up monthly payments for the duration of the rental period. Make sure to keep track of any payments that have been made and provide receipts when requested.

7. Maintain the Rent Space: Lastly, you should make sure to maintain the Rent Space while it is being rented out. This includes making any necessary repairs and keeping the area clean and tidy.

By following these steps, you can successfully rent out a parking space. Renting a parking space can be a great way to generate additional income while also providing people with a much-needed service.

Advantage Of Rent Out A Parking Space

Renting out your parking space can be a great way to make some extra money. Renting out your parking space can help you offset the costs of keeping and maintaining it while also providing you with an additional source of income. Renters may also be more likely to take care of the area than if they were using it for free, meaning that you can expect your parking space to stay in good condition. Renting out your parking spot also provides an opportunity for renters who may not have access to other forms of transportation, such as those without a car or those who are looking for a more convenient way to get around. Renters may also be willing to pay a premium price for the convenience and security of your parking space. Renting out a parking space can also be beneficial for you in terms of tax purposes. Depending on the country or area that you live in, you may be able to claim rent as an expense, which can help reduce your tax liability. Renting out a parking space can also provide peace of mind for both parties, guaranteeing that your property won't be abused or misused. Overall, renting out a parking space can benefit both yourself and the renter. It can be a great way to make some extra money while also providing convenience for those who need it.

The Disadvantages Of Rent Out A Parking Space

Renting out a parking space can be beneficial in terms of additional income, but there are also downsides to consider. Renters may not always pay their rent on time or in full, which could leave you with lost revenue. You'll also need to set up a contract to outline the rules and expectations between yourself and your tenant, which can be time-consuming. Renters may also bring their own liability and insurance to the space, so you'll need to ensure that these are up-to-date and within the terms of your agreement. Finally, you'll be responsible for the space's maintenance and any necessary repairs, which could involve extra financial costs. All of these potential issues should be considered before deciding to rent a parking space.

Overall, Renting out a parking space can bring in additional income and provide flexibility for your tenants, but there are potential drawbacks that should be considered before taking on this venture. It's important to weigh the pros and cons and decide what is best for you and your property. Renting out a parking space can provide a great opportunity for both parties, but make sure you know what is involved before signing any contracts or agreements.

Tips For Rent Out A Parking Space

1. Research the local market: Before renting out your parking space, research the local market to understand what other landlords are charging for similar spaces in your area. This will help you determine a fair rental rate and ensure that you're getting a reasonable return on your investment.

2. Advertise your space: Reach out to potential renters with an ad describing the features of your space. Be sure to include any amenities or conveniences, such as a security gate or proximity to public transportation, that may draw more attention and potentially increase the rental rate.

3. Offer incentives: Renters may be more likely to sign a lease if you offer incentives such as discounted rates for longer leases or a month-to-month agreement. You can also offer discounts to tenants who pay their rent on time.

4. Prepare the space: Before renting out your parking space, ensure it is in safe and good condition by carrying out any necessary repairs or maintenance work. Additionally, be sure to clearly mark the boundaries of your space with paint or other materials.

5. Draft a contract: A written lease agreement is

essential when renting out a parking space and should include details such as the rental rate, length of lease, payment terms, and any additional rules that tenants must agree to follow. Be sure to consult with an attorney if you have any questions or concerns.

6. Collect payment: Renters should know when and how to pay their rent upon signing the lease agreement. Be sure to collect payment on time and in full each month to avoid any potential issues or disputes.

By following these tips, you'll be well on your way to renting out a parking space and earning a passive income. With the right approach, you can make money while offering an invaluable service to tenants in your area.

Rent Out Your Home For Short-Term

Rent out your home short-term to make some extra money. Whether you're looking to cover the costs of a mortgage or just want to turn your property into a side hustle, renting out your home can be an easy and lucrative way to make some extra cash. From setting up with Airbnb, HomeAway, or VRBO to considering local regulations and taxes, there are plenty of important factors to consider when renting out your home.

You'll need to research local tax laws to pay all required taxes on rental income. You'll also look into any applicable zoning restrictions and homeowner association rules to ensure you don't run afoul of any regulations. Finally, setting up insurance coverage for a short-term rental is important. Most homeowners policies won't cover any liability, so you may need to purchase additional coverage.

What Are The Steps For Starting Rent Out Your Home Short-Term ?

1. Determine Your Needs: Before considering short-term, make sure it's the right move for you. Next, assess your lifestyle and needs to determine whether or not this is something that would fit into your daily life.

2. Check Local Regulations: Make sure to check local regulations about what's allowed in your area. Some municipalities have bans on short-term rental activity, or may require special permits and fees for you to operate legally.

3. Renting Platforms: Once you've checked your local regulations, look ifferent renting platformre like Airbnb and HomeAway that are available to help you rent out your home.

4. Setting Rent Prices: Decide how much you want

to charge per night and develop a pricing strategy that's competitive yet still profitable. Keep in mind that you will need to factor in taxes, fees, and any additional costs associated with short-term rentals.

5. Prepare Your Home: Make sure that your home is clean and comfortable for renters. Consider making industry repairs or upgrades, as well as stocking essentials like fresh linens and toiletries.

6. Promote Your Renting Space: Once you have everything set up, it's time to start advertising your rental space. Again, use social media, forums, websites, and other methods to get the word out and attract potential renters.

With these steps, you can start Renting out your home short-term. Renters will appreciate the convenience of having a place that is ready for them and you'll enjoy the financial benefits of renting out your space.

Advantage Of Rent Out Your Home Short-Term

Renting out your home on a short-term basis can be a great way to supplement your income and make use of your property when you're not there. Renting out your home through Airbnb, HomeAway, or other vacation rental sites can bring in more money than traditional long-term rentals. Renters may also be able to benefit from tax breaks and other incentives from their local governments. Additionally, renting out your home short-term can be a great way to meet people from all over the world who may have different perspectives and experiences than you. Renting out your property is also much quicker and less hassle than traditional long-term rentals, as it's usually just a matter of setting up an account on a vacation rental site and listing your property. Finally, it can be fun to meet new people and find out about different cultures when renting out your home short-term. Renting out your home through Airbnb or other vacation rental sites can provide you with extra income, broaden your horizons, and make use of your space when you're not there. It's worth considering for anyone looking to supplement their income and make new connections.

The Disadvantage Of Rent Out Your Home Short-Term

Rent out your home short-term is that it may not be as profitable as long-term rental. You need to take into account the cost of maintenance and taxes, as well as other fees associated with renting out a property. In addition, you may have difficulty finding renters if you are in an area with high demand, which can limit your potential income. Renting out a home short-term also requires more to find renters actively as you need to find renters and manage their stay actively. Finally, there is the risk of damage to your property if something goes on during a short-term rental. All of these factors can reduce the potential return on investment you main the short term from renting out your home short-term.

The Tips For Rent Out Your Home Short-Term

Renting out your home short-term can be a great way to generate some extra income. Here are some tips for getting the most out of it:

1. Make sure you do your research on local laws and regulations regarding short-term rentals. Many cities have restrictions or rules that must be followed in order to rent out your home legally.

2. Develop a rental agreement that outlines your expectations and the terms of the rental. This can help ensure a smooth rental experience for both you and the renter.

3. Consider offering amenities that will make your rental more attractive to potential renters, such as high-speed internet access or cable television.

4. Make sure your rental space is clean, secure and in good repair before letting any renters in.

5. Advertise your rental on popular websites like

Airbnb or VRBO to get the most exposure for your listing.

6. Screen potential renters thoroughly to make sure they're trustworthy and reliable. You can ask for references or even require a background check if you feel it is necessary.

7. Set reasonable rates for your rental that are in line with the area. You want to make sure you're getting fair compensation for the rental without pricing yourself out of the market.

With careful planning and research, renting out your home short-term can be a great way to supplement your income. Just remember to follow the laws and regulations regarding short-term rentals in your area, screen potential renters thoroughly, and be mindful of other safety concerns.

CHAPER

8 :INVESING

R EITs
(Real Estate Investment Trusts) are an
important tool for investors looking to
diversify their portfolios and gain exposure to
real estate. REITs provide access to commercial
properties such as office buildings, hotels, and
apartment complexes. REITs allow investors to
benefit from the potential appreciation of a
property without having to buy it outright or
manage it themselves. REITs are also attractive
investments because they offer a steady stream of
income from rental and other fees associated with
the properties that make up their portfolios. REITs
offer investors a variety of benefits, including
portfolio diversification, inflation protection, and
tax advantages. REITs can offer higher yields than
many traditional fixed-income investments like

bonds or CDs, making them attractive to investors in search of yield. REITs can also provide exposure to international real estate markets, which may not be available with traditional investments. REITs are a popular investment option for retirement accounts, as they often offer higher yields than other fixed-income investments while providing tax advantages and diversification benefits. REITs can be a great way to diversify and add stability to an investment portfolio. REITs are also a great option for those looking for long-term capital gains, as REITs have the potential to appreciate over time. REITs offer investors the chance to invest in real estate without having to go through the hassle of actively managing properties themselves. REITs provide liquidity, as they can be easily bought and sold on public markets. REITs are also a great option for those just getting started in investing, as REITs have relatively low entry costs compared to other investments, such as stocks or mutual funds.

What Are The Steps For Starting Reits?

Starting REITs involves several steps.

1. Understand REITs: REITs are a type of

investment vehicle that invests in income-producing real estate. REITs can provide investors with higher returns than many other asset classes, as well as greater diversification and liquidity.

2. Determine your REIT investment strategy: REITs can be used to pursue a variety of investment strategies, such as income generation, capital appreciation, or risk management. Before investing in REITs, it is important to consider your goals and objectives.

3. Choose REITs: There are many different REITs available for investors to choose from, including REITs that invest in different types of real estates, such as residential, commercial, industrial, and hospitality. It is important to research REITs before investing in order to understand the type of investments and risk factors associated with them.

4. Set up an account: To buy REITs, you will need to set up an account with a financial institution. When choosing an account, compare different fees, services, and features to select one that best suits your REIT strategy.

5. Purchase REITs: After selecting REITs for a portfolio, it is time to purchase them. REITs can be bought on a stock exchange or through an online broker. It is important to research REITs thoroughly before investing and diversify your REIT investments to manage risk.

6. Monitor REIT Performance: After purchasing REITs, it is important to monitor the performance of your investments on a regular basis. This will allow you to make necessary adjustments to ensure REITs are performing as expected and meeting your investment goals.

By following these steps, investors can start investing in REITs with confidence. REITs can be a great way to diversify an investment portfolio and provide long-term returns. However, it is essential to research REITs thoroughly before investing and to monitor REIT performance regularly in order to maximize returns.

Advantage Of Reits

Real Estate Investment Trusts (REITs) offer a way for investors to gain access to the real estate market without having to own physical real estate. REITs are a type of security that pools the money of many investors and invests in real estate-related assets such as mortgages, properties, and other real estate investments. REITs offer unique advantages to investors as they are liquid assets with the potential for high returns and dividends. REITs also provide diversification of investment portfolios and can be used to create a balanced portfolio. In addition, REITs can be traded on an exchange like stocks, which makes them even more accessible than owning physical real estate. REITs can also be tax efficient as they are typically structured to minimize taxes, allowing investors to take advantage of the favourable tax treatment available to REITs.

The Disadvantages Of Reits

the disadvantages of include their lack of liquidity, as REITs are typically traded on stock exchanges and are not always easy to buy or sell. Additionally, REITs may be highly vulnerable to market changes and can be more volatile than other investments. REITs also tend to pay out a large portion of their income as dividends, which means that the holdings may not appreciate in value as much as other investments. As REITs are subject to certain tax regulations, investors must be aware of the potential consequences of investing in REITs. Finally, REITs can also require up-front costs, such as commissions and fees, that may hinder long-term returns.

Tips For Reits

investors

1. Understand REITs: REITs are Real Estate Investment Trusts, allowing investors to participate in the ownership of commercial real estate assets without purchasing property

directly. REITs offer the potential for higher returns than traditional investments such as stocks or bonds and can be a good choice for diversifying an investment portfolio. Before investing in REITs, it is important to understand the types of REITs available, how they work, and the associated risks.

2. Research REITs: There are many REITs available on the market today, so it is important to do your research to find one that matches your investment goals and objectives. Consider factors such as REIT size, type of property owned, historical performance, and management team when making your selection.

3. Diversify Your REIT Portfolio: REITs can be a great way to diversify an investment portfolio. In addition, investing in multiple REITs helps spread risk across different sectors, which can help reduce the overall risk of your portfolio.

4. Monitor REIT Performance: REITs are subject to market conditions, so it is important to monitor their performance over time and make adjustments as necessary. Pay close attention to economic news and trends in the real estate market that could impact REIT performance.

5. Consider REIT Investing Strategies: A variety of REIT investing strategies can be used to maximize returns and minimize risk. For example, some investors may choose to invest in REITs that focus

on specific sectors or geographic regions, while others may opt for REITs with higher dividends. Taking the time to understand REIT investing strategies can help you make the most of REIT investing.

By understanding REITs, researching REITs available on the market, diversifying REIT investments, and considering REIT investing strategies, investors can make informed decisions about REIT investing and potentially realize higher returns than other traditional investments. With careful research and monitoring, REIT investments can be a great way to diversify a portfolio and reap the rewards of real estate investing.

A Bond Ladder

A bond ladder is an investing strategy designed to achieve a balanced mix of security, yield, and liquidity. It involves buying bonds with varying maturities that all produce income at regular intervals. By staggering the maturities in equal amounts, investors can diversify their portfolios and create steady cash flows over time. A bond ladder also allows them to take advantage of rising interest rates since they are able to reinvest their maturing bonds at the current rate. A bond ladder is a great way for investors to balance risk and reward, while still keeping an eye on liquidity needs. It's important to remember that the longer a bond's maturity, the higher its yield will be, and the greater its risk. A bond ladder helps to diversify across maturities, which can lower risk and provide a steady income stream. By creating a balanced bond portfolio with a ladder strategy, investors can enjoy the potential for higher returns while still maintaining liquidity.

What Are The Steps For Starting A Bond Ladder?

Creating a bond ladder effectively builds wealth over time and reduces risk in your portfolio. A bond ladder consists of buying multiple bonds at various maturity dates, so that you have bonds maturing at regular intervals (e.g. every three months). This allows you to reinvest your capital periodically and keep your portfolio's average rate of return at a more consistent level.

The steps for starting A bond ladder are as follows:

1. Determine Your Investment Goal – Before you begin building your bond ladder, determine what type of return you want to achieve and what kind of risk you're willing to take on.

2. Choose the Bond Types and Quantities – Decide on the types of bonds you're going to invest in, such as Treasury bonds, municipal bonds or corporate bonds. Also, consider the quantity of

each type of bond you'll need to purchase.

3. Calculate the Maturity Dates – Determine how often you want your ladder to mature by calculating when the bonds will reach their maturity dates.

4. Allocate Your Investment Funds – Take the money you've saved for investing and allocate it to purchase the bonds in your ladder.

5. Monitor Your Bond Ladder Regularly – Once you have created your bond ladder, you should monitor its performance regularly to ensure that it is still meeting your investment goals.

By following these steps, you can create an effective bond ladder that will help you achieve your long-term financial goals. A bond ladder is a great way to secure and grow your wealth over time while minimizing risk in the process.

Advantage Of A Bond Ladder

A bond ladder is a strategy for investing in fixed income that provides investors with regular and predictable returns. A bond ladder can help minimize risk by diversifying investments across multiple bonds and providing the ability to invest periodically over time. Bond ladders also provide flexibility, allowing investors to purchase longer-term bonds when interest rates are low or shorter-term bonds when interest rates are high. Bond ladders can also provide regular cash flows as each bond matures, allowing investors to reinvest the proceeds at a higher interest rate if desired. A bond ladder is an efficient way to manage fixed-income investments while providing diversification and flexibility. By investing in multiple bonds over time, investors can take advantage of the changing interest rate environment and create a portfolio that meets their risk tolerance and return objectives. A bond ladder may be an ideal strategy for those who are looking to maintain regular cash flows and minimize risk.

The Disadvantages Of A Bond Ladder

The main disadvantage of a bond ladder is that it requires investors to have large upfront capital. A bond ladder typically requires all the bonds to be purchased upfront, which can be a significant expense for many investors. Additionally, since bonds are generally priced according to the current market conditions, there is no guarantee of making a profit from your investments. A bond ladder also requires investors to be knowledgeable about the various market conditions that can affect its performance. A lack of knowledge in this area could result in losses for investors if they make an incorrect decision. Finally, while a bond ladder provides a reliable income stream, it may not always outperform alternative investments, such as stocks and mutual funds, over the long term. As a result, investors should carefully consider their individual goals before committing to such an investment strategy.

Overall, A bond ladder is a great way to diversify investments and maximize returns over the long term. Some disadvantages must be considered when deciding if this strategy is right for you. Understanding the risks associated with A bond ladder and having the necessary knowledge to make informed decisions. With this knowledge, A bond ladder can be a great addition to your portfolio.

Tips For A Bond Ladder

A bond ladder is an investment strategy where a portfolio of bonds of different maturities and credit ratings is purchased to provide income and capital preservation. A bond ladder can serve as a way to diversify a fixed-income portfolio and spread out the risk associated with investing in bonds.

Creating an effective bond ladder requires carefully considering your financial goals and the current market environment. Here are some tips to help you build a successful bond ladder:

1. Choose A Diversified Mix of Bonds - A

bond ladder should include bonds with different maturities and credit ratings in order to spread out risks associated with investing in fixed-income securities. A diversified mix of bonds helps minimize the impact of any single bond or market event.

2. Consider A Ladder Of Different Maturities - A bond ladder should include bonds with different maturities in order to take advantage of changing interest rates. A mix of short-term and longer-term bonds can help adjust your portfolio to rising and falling rates without completely reinvesting your money.

3. Consider A Ladder Of Different Ratings - A bond ladder should also include bonds with different credit ratings in order to manage risk and reward. For example, lower-rated bonds offer higher yields but can be more volatile, while higher-rated bonds are typically safer investments but may not offer as much potential return.

4. Rebalance Your Ladder Regularly - A bond ladder should be regularly reviewed and rebalanced to ensure it remains true to your financial goals. As bonds mature, they can be replaced with new bonds that fit the requirements of your investment strategy. This helps diversify your portfolio and allows you to take advantage of changing interest rates.

By following these tips, you can create an effective

bond ladder that meets your financial goals and helps manage risk. A well-constructed bond ladder is a great way to invest in fixed-income securities without taking on too much risk.

Bank

Invest in a high-yield CD or savings account

Invest in a high-yield CD or savings account to maximize the amount of money you can earn from your savings. Investing in a CD or savings account is an excellent way to get the most out of your money, as these types of accounts provide higher yields than traditional banking products. With a high-yield account, you'll be able to earn more interest on your funds and grow your savings faster. Investing in a CD or savings account also offers security since these accounts are FDIC insured against loss of principal. Investing in a high-yield CD or savings account is an easy and accessible way for anyone to begin growing their wealth and investing for the future. Investing in one of these accounts can help you meet your short-term or long-term financial goals. Investing in a high-yield CD or savings account can also provide you with peace of mind, knowing that your funds are safe and secure. With the right choices, investing in a high-yield CD or

savings account can be an important step towards achieving your financial dreams. Invest today, and watch your savings grow! Investing in a CD or savings account is a safe, secure way to make the most of your hard-earned money.

What Are The Steps For Starting Invest In A High-Yield Cd Or Savings Account?

Investing in a high-yield certificate of deposit (CD) or savings account can be a great way to grow your money, and the process is simple. Here's how you get started:

1. Shop around: Investigate different banks and financial institutions to compare rates, terms, minimum balance requirements, and fees.

2. Choose the best option: Consider the benefits of each institution and select the CD or savings account that best meets your financial needs.

3. Open an account: When you're ready, open a new CD or savings account with the bank or financial institution of your choice. This process typically requires some basic information about yourself and your financial goals.

4. Make a deposit: Most institutions require you to make an initial deposit in order to open the account. The exact amount may vary depending

on the institution, so read all the details before making a decision.

5. Monitor your progress: Investing in a high-yield CD or savings account is a long-term investment. Monitor your progress over time to ensure that you're on track to meet your financial goals.

The Advantage Of Invest In A High-Yield Cd Or Savings Account

is that it provides higher returns than traditional savings accounts, making them an excellent option for those looking to maximize their savings. Investing in a high-yield CD or savings account is generally considered to be low-risk and relatively safe compared to other types of investments. The interest earned on your investment will also depend on the term length you choose - with longer-term investments typically yielding a higher return. Investing in a high-yield CD or savings account is also an incredibly flexible option, with no minimum deposits and the ability to withdraw your funds whenever you need them without penalty. Investing in a high-yield CD or savings account is an excellent way to build wealth over time without exposing yourself to too much risk. Investing in a high-yield CD or savings account also allows you to earn compound interest, meaning that you can earn even more money over time simply by letting your investment grow and collecting the associated interest payments.

The Disadvantage Of Invest In A High-Yield Cd Or Savings Account

is that it is not as liquid as other investments. This means that you cannot access your money whenever and however you want to. To withdraw funds from a CD or savings account, you may incur penalties or need to wait for the CD to mature. Additionally, you might need help finding a financial institution willing to offer a high-yield option with a small deposit amount. Investing in a high-yield CD or savings account can also be risky if your chosen financial institution is unstable. Finally, the rate of return on these investments may not keep up with inflation, meaning that your money might not have as much buying power over time as it does initially. There may be better options than investing in a high-yield CD or savings account for those with short-term goals. Investing in a high-yield CD or savings account can also be difficult to track and manage if you have multiple accounts at different financial institutions. Finally, investing in a high-yield CD or savings account is often considered a low-risk investment, but that may not always be the case. Investing in a high-yield CD or savings account can be risky if the financial institution you choose is unstable. So it is important to research financial institutions thoroughly before investing your money.

Stake Cryptocurrencies

Stake cryptocurrencies are an alternative way to make money in the cryptocurrency world compared to traditional trading. This involves leaving your assets with a reliable platform and earning rewards based on the amount of coins you have staked. Staking coins gives investors more control over their crypto holdings as they can decide when and how much to invest instead of being at the mercy of market fluctuations. Staking also allows users to earn rewards through block production, which is more passive income than other investing methods. Staking has become increasingly popular in recent years due to its potential for high returns and low risk. Stakers can look forward to regular dividend payments from the staking platform, as well as appreciation in value over time as the price of the staked coins rises. Staking is a great option for those who want to invest in cryptocurrency without actively managing their portfolio or being at the mercy of market fluctuations. Stake cryptocurrencies can be a good idea if you're looking for long-term passive income and are comfortable with some risk. It's important to do your research and find a reliable platform to stake with before investing. Staking can be risky, but it also offers the potential for high rewards if done correctly. Stake cryptocurrencies are definitely an option worth considering if you're looking to make passive income with your cryptocurrency investments.

What Are The Steps For Starting Stake Cryptocurrencies?

Staking cryptocurrencies is the process of locking away a certain amount of coins for a specified period of time in order to earn rewards. Staking can be done through an exchange or a staking service provider, depending on the specific cryptocurrency.

To get started with staking, you will need to choose the cryptocurrency you want to stake and the exchange or Staking service provider you will use. Once you've made your choice, you will need to register an account with the chosen Staking service provider or exchange. After registering, you will transfer your desired amount of cryptocurrency into your Staking wallet and then start staking.

The process of Staking will vary depending on the Staking service provider or exchange you are using as well as how long you plan to Stake for. Generally, Staking rewards will be paid out periodically, such as every month or quarter.

Once you have Staked your cryptocurrency, it is important to keep track of the Staking rewards you receive and any changes in Staking requirements. Staked cryptocurrencies may also be subject to taxes, so you should check with your local taxation office for more information regarding applicable tax rates.

Advantage Of Stake Cryptocurrencies

is the ease of use compared to other forms of passive investing. Staking does not require a large upfront investment and can be done with as little as one single cryptocurrency. Staking also offers potential rewards in the form of coins and tokens, which may increase in value over time if the underlying asset appreciates. Staking also requires less maintenance than other forms of passive investing as it does not require the investor to monitor and manage their investments actively. Staked assets also tend to be more secure than other investment forms since they are held in a decentralized blockchain network rather than vulnerable centralized exchanges. Finally, staking can provide investors with additional liquidity that is not available with other forms of investing, allowing them to liquidate their holdings much more quickly and cheaply. Stake cryptocurrencies offer investors a unique opportunity to benefit from the potential upside of cryptos without having to be actively involved in trading or managing investments. By staking digital assets, investors can earn rewards while taking on minimal risk, making it an attractive option for diversifying their portfolio and adding passive income to their financial plan.

The Disadvantage Of Stake Cryptocurrencies

as a passive income idea is the volatility of the cryptocurrency market. Staking with cryptocurrencies may be a great way to earn some extra money, but it can also be quite a risky endeavour. Staked coins may rapidly increase in value, but they can also quickly lose their value due to market volatility or the lack of liquidity. Staking with cryptocurrencies, therefore, can be a high-risk venture and should only be done by those who are comfortable taking on that risk. Additionally, one must be aware that staked coins can't be sold or traded. At the same time, they are locked up in the staking process, meaning that they are effectively removed from the market and unavailable to be used as a form of payment or exchange. Lastly, some exchanges impose restrictions on staking, meaning that not all cryptocurrencies may be available for staking with them. Stake cryptocurrencies should only be done by those who understand their risks and potential rewards. Staking can yield great returns, but it can also lead to significant losses. Investors must understand the potential risks before investing to ensure that Staking with cryptocurrencies is a decision they are comfortable with making.

Tips For Stake Cryptocurrencies As Passive Income

Staking cryptocurrency is one of the most popular ways to earn a passive income. Staking cryptocurrency involves holding crypto coins in a designated wallet and using them as collateral to validate transactions on the network and receive rewards for doing so. Staking your coins allows you to earn rewards without actively trading or monitoring markets. Staking also helps secure the network, making it more reliable and efficient. Staking is a great way to build up your portfolio without taking big risks. Staking also requires much less time and effort than actively trading cryptocurrencies and can generate steady returns over time. Staking is becoming increasingly popular among investors who want to diversify their portfolios with passive income-generating cryptocurrencies. Staking can be done with a variety of cryptocurrencies, including Bitcoin, Ethereum, Ripple, and many more. Before staking your cryptocurrency, it is important to research the network and understand the associated risks. Stacking requires users to hold their coins in designated wallets for extended periods, so it is important to ensure you are comfortable with doing so. Staking is a great way to earn passive income from your cryptocurrency investments and can be a lucrative long-term strategy if done correctly. Stacking requires patience and research but can be an effective way to generate a steady source of income over time.

Robo Investing

Robo Investing is an increasingly popular form of passive income. Robo-investing uses technology to automate the process of building and managing a diversified portfolio with minimal effort from investors. Robo-advisors such as Betterment, Wealthfront, and Acorns use algorithms to build portfolios that are tailored to each investor's individual risk tolerance, time horizon, investment goals, and financial situation. Robo-investing can help investors save money on trading fees, minimize their risk of loss due to market volatility, and reduce the amount of time required for portfolio management. Robo-investing is a great way for both experienced and novice investors to take advantage of passive income opportunities without sacrificing potential returns. Robo Investing also provides a convenient platform for those without the time or expertise to manage their investments actively. With Robo Investing, investors can take a hands-off approach and still enjoy the potential for long-term growth. Robo investing is becoming increasingly popular among those looking for passive income streams that require minimal effort and provide steady returns. Robo investing can be important in diversifying a portfolio and creating a passive income stream. Robo Investing is a great way for investors to diversify their portfolio and easily generate income. Robo investing requires minimal effort and provides the potential for long-term growth, making it an attractive option for those seeking passive income streams.

What Are The Steps For Starting Robo Investing?

Robo Investing is an automated, low-cost option for diversifying their investments and creating a passive income source. Here are the steps for getting started:

1. Understand Your Risk Tolerance: Robo Investing involves managing your own portfolio in the stock market, which can be risky depending on what stocks you choose and how much you invest. It's important to determine your own risk tolerance before investing in any Robo Investing platform.

2. Research Robo Investing Platforms: There are a variety of Robo Investing platforms available, and it's important to find one that meets your needs. Research each platform carefully, including fees, minimum investments, and any other criteria.

3. Set Up Your Robo Investing Account: Once you've chosen a Robo Investing platform, you'll then need to set up your account. This includes providing personal information as well as linking an outside bank account for transferring funds.

4. Create an Investment Plan: Robo Investing platforms allow you to choose the stocks, ETFs and other investments that make up your portfolio. Determine how much risk you wish to take on and which type of investment will best meet your goals.

5. Monitor Regularly: Robo Investing requires regular monitoring to ensure your portfolio is performing as expected. Keep an eye on market activity, check your Robo Investing account, and make adjustments as needed.

The Advantage Of Robo Investing

Robo Investing is that it eliminates much of the work and stress associated with stock market investing. Robo Investing is a passive income stream, meaning you don't have to manage your investments actively—the software does it for you. Robo Investing automates everything from finding suitable investments to making trades at the right time. This can help investors make better decisions and reduce the chances of making costly mistakes. Robo Investing also allows investors to diversify their portfolios with minimal effort, as it can identify a variety of investments that meet their needs. Robo Investing also helps minimize risk by allowing investors to control their exposure to different markets and asset classes. Finally, Robo Investing is an easy way for people to start investing with little or no upfront cost, meaning they can build their nest egg without worrying about large investments. Robo Investing offers investors a unique opportunity to benefit from the stock market with minimal effort and risk.

The Disadvantage Of Robo Investing

is that it can be quite expensive. Robo Investing services usually charge a fee for their services, which can range from 0.25% to 2% of the amount you invest each year. This fee is in addition to any fees associated with buying and selling individual investments. Additionally, Robo Investing does not provide personalized advice or recommendations tailored to your specific financial situation. Robo Investing services may also have limited investment options, which can limit the potential returns on your investments.

For these reasons, Robo Investing is not always ideal for everyone and should be carefully considered before investing. Ultimately, Robo Investing is best suited for those who are comfortable with the risks involved and confident in their ability to manage their own investments. Robo Investing can be a great way to build wealth passively, but it is important to understand the potential risks and rewards before investing.

Another disadvantage of Robo Investing is that it requires you to have a certain level of financial literacy in order to use the service effectively. Robo Investing services usually provide basic educational materials to help you become more familiar with investing, but Robo Investing is not suitable for those who lack financial knowledge or experience. Therefore, if you are considering Robo Investing as a way to build wealth passively, it is important to ensure that you are adequately prepared and understand the risks involved.

Tips Of The Advantage Of Robo Investing

Robo Investing allows investors to gain passive income through investing in a wide variety of stocks and securities. Robo Investing allows for diversified portfolios and automated decisions and can be tailored to meet individual investor needs. Robo Investing also offers lower fees than human brokers or financial advisors and provides 24/7 access to accounts. Robo Investing is often viewed as a lower-risk option for investors, due to its automated decisions and the ability to diversify investments easily. Additionally, Robo Investing can be tailored to fit individual investor needs and portfolios by providing personalized investment advice based on an individual's particular financial situation. Robo Investing also eliminates the need for costly broker fees and allows for more flexibility in terms of investment decisions, allowing investors to have greater control over their investments. Finally, Robo Investing makes it easy and convenient to manage your portfolio with little effort on the part of the investor. As a result, Robo Investing can be a great way to achieve passive income while also reducing risk and increasing returns.

With Robo Investing, you can create a passive income stream by leveraging the power of automated technology. As long as you understand your risk tolerance, research Robo Investing platforms carefully and choose an investment plan that suits you, Robo Investing can be a great way to grow your wealth.

Invest In Vending Machines

Investing in vending machines is one of the most passive ideas to make money. Investing in vending machines allows you to set up your own business without having to do any of the work associated with managing a traditional brick-and-mortar store. Instead, you can purchase a vending machine and install it in high-traffic locations. From there, all you have to do is keep it stocked with products, collect money, and you're ready to make a profit. Investing in vending machines is also a great way to diversify your income portfolio and add another passive income stream. Investing in the right vending machines can be highly profitable, so it's important to research before investing in a machine. Investing in different types of vending machines allows you to find the right combination that works best for your particular location. Researching and understanding the different aspects of investing in vending machines will help you make an informed decision when it comes time to decide which type of machine is right for you.

What Are The Steps For Starting Invest In Vending Machines?

Investing in vending machines can be a lucrative way to earn extra income, but it takes some effort and knowledge. Before you start investing in vending machines, there are several steps you need to take.

The first step is to do your research. First,

investigate the different types of vending machines available, their features, and the areas they serve. Next, investigate the businesses in your area that have the most potential for success, and research what products they typically offer. This can help you decide which type of machine best suits your location.

Once you've narrowed down the type of machine you'd like to purchase, it's time to start looking at prices and seeing what kind of deals you can get. Investing in vending machines means buying used or refurbished machines, so be sure to consider the quality of the machine and its condition before you commit to a purchase.

The next step is to select a location for your business. This could mean renting space in a mall or shopping centre, renting space near an existing business, or even setting up your own shop. Next, investigate your chosen location's zoning rules and regulations to see if you're allowed to install a vending machine there.

Once you've found a suitable space, it's time to purchase or rent a vending machine. Look for one that is easy to use, has a variety of products, and is reliable. Invest in a machine that will give you a good return on investment, which is important to successful vending operations.

Finally, it's time to stock your machine and begin operations. Research the most popular snack items in your area and source them from reliable suppliers at competitive prices. Invest in marketing materials and promotional campaigns to draw in customers and make sure your machine stands out

Advantage Of Invest In Vending Machines

is that you can generate a steady stream of income passively. Investing in vending machines is ideal for establishing a business with minimal effort and start-up costs. You can purchase an existing machine and set up shop almost immediately, or you can rent space for your vending machine in high-traffic areas to ensure you get the most out of your investment. With minimal overhead costs and minimal maintenance, you can easily generate an income without spending more time or money. Investing in vending machines is a great way to get into the passive income game and start making money with minimal effort. Investing in vending machines can also provide you with the opportunity to diversify your portfolio and increase your income potential. With the right location and quality products, you can turn a small investment into a profitable venture that will pay dividends for years to come. Investing in vending machines is an ideal way to start building wealth without having to worry about managing and maintaining multiple businesses.

The Disadvantage Of Invest In Vending Machines

Investing in vending machines can seem like a passive income opportunity, but it comes with its own risks. Investing in vending machines requires an up-front investment that may not be recoverable if the machine does not perform as expected. Additionally, you must consider other factors such as location, maintenance costs, and theft or vandalism when deciding whether to invest in vending machines. Investing in vending machines requires a long-term commitment, and you may find yourself stuck with a machine that is not performing as expected or has become obsolete due to technological changes. Furthermore, you will need to monitor your machine's performance continually, ensuring it is stocked with goods and prices are kept up to date. Investing in vending machines can be risky, but with careful planning and research, it can also be rewarding. Investing in vending machines requires commitment and dedication to ensure that the machine performs well and generates a steady income.

Tips For Invest In Vending Machines

Investing in vending machines can be a great way to make money and have passive income. With the right planning, you can earn steady revenue from your vending machines with minimal effort or expenses. Here are some tips for investing in vending machines:

1. Choose the Right Machines: Invest in high-quality, reliable vending machines that are well-made and low maintenance. Investing in a good machine can help you maximize your profits by ensuring it is always stocked and running smoothly.

2. Choose High-Traffic Locations: Investing in vending machines that are located in areas with high foot traffic will allow you to get more customers and increase your revenue potential. Consider places like malls, office buildings, or other public spaces that receive a lot of visitors.

3. Invest in Stock: Investing in stock for your vending machines can help you maximize your profits by selling more items and reducing the number of times you need to restock each machine. In addition, investing in a good stock selection will ensure that customers always have something to choose from.

4. Invest in Advertising: Advertising can help you draw more customers to your vending machines and increase revenue potential. Consider ways to advertise, such as placing flyers or signs around the location of your vending machines, running ads online, or partnering with local businesses to promote each other's services.

By following these tips, you can make the most out of your investment in vending machines and enjoy a steady stream of passive income. Investing in vending machines can be an excellent way to earn money and create passive revenue with minimal effort.

CHAPER 9 : SOCIAL MEDIA AND MARKETING

reate a blog or YouTube channel
Create a blog or YouTube channel as a passive income idea. With the rise of digital media, blogs and YouTube channels are becoming increasingly popular ways for people to make money online. You can create content about anything that interests you or use your existing knowledge to educate others on topics you're passionate about. Depending on how much time you put into it and the type of content you create, you can make money from your blog or channel through ads, sponsorships, and affiliate programs.

Plus, it's a great way to network with other bloggers and influencers in your niche. So create a blog or YouTube channel today and start making money as you share your passions with the world!

Making takes more effort the channel does take more effort than some other passive income options. You need to create quality content regularly and invest in marketing your channel or blog effectively. However, the rewards can be well worth it. With a successful blog or YouTube channel, you could make enough money to quit your day job and work from home full-time! So create a blog or YouTube channel today and start making money with your passions.

Creating a blog or YouTube channel as a passive income option is an excellent way to make money doing something that you love. You can create content about anything that interests you and use it to educate others while also making some extra cash on the side. Take the time to research your niche, create great content, and market it effectively to start seeing what rewards of your hard work.

What Are The Steps For Starting To Create A Blog Or Youtube Channel?

If you're interested in creating a blog or YouTube channel to generate passive income, here are the steps you need to take:

1. Choose Your Platform - First, decide which platform (blogging or YouTube) is the best fit for your content. If you're comfortable speaking and recording videos, then YouTube might be the best option. On the other hand, if you're not comfortable on camera but can write, then blogging might be better for you.

2. Create a Strategy - Before starting your blog or YouTube channel, think about your target audience and what type of content you want to create. This will help you create content that resonates with your audience and is valuable to them.

3. Create Quality Content - Once you've chosen a platform and created a strategy, it's time to start creating content. Make sure that the content you create is high quality, interesting, and helpful for your target audience. It's also important to stay consistent in order to build an audience and drive engagement.

4. Promote Your Content - Once you've created your content, it's time to promote it! Create social media accounts on the major platforms and use them to share your content. You can also reach out to influencers in your niche and ask them to share

or link to your content.

5. Create an Income Stream - Once your content starts getting traction, you can start to think about ways to generate income from it. For example, create products or services related to your blog or channel, and find ways to monetize the traffic that comes in.

Advantage Of Creating A Blog Or Youtube Channel

is that it can generate passive income. With the right understanding of SEO, content optimization, and internet marketing, you can turn creating a blog or YouTube channel into a business. You have complete control over what type of content goes on these platforms and you can monetize them with advertisements. You could also use affiliate links to generate revenue from your posts or videos. This is a great way to make money on the side without putting in too much effort. You can also build an audience and potentially increase your visibility, allowing for more opportunities down the line. Creating a blog or YouTube channel can effectively generate passive income and reach potential customers. Furthermore, it gives you a platform to express yourself, share your ideas and connect with others. By becoming an authority in a certain field, you can build trust and credibility with your audience and gain access to more valuable resources. Overall, creating a blog or YouTube channel is a great way to start making money online without any major overhead costs. It gives you the freedom to work on your own terms, build your own brand, and reach a wider audience.

The Disadvantages Of Creating A Blog Or Youtube Channel

The main disadvantage of creating a blog or YouTube channel as a passive income idea is a cost and time involved. Creating content, promoting it, and maintaining it can be costly in terms of money and time. Additionally, there is no guarantee that your content will become popular or that you must ensure that you provide the content that your audience will find. Furthermore, plagiarism or copyright infringement is always possible if you do not take proper precautions when using other people's material in your content. Finally, it is taking on such a passive income idea. Ultimately, it can be a rewarding experience if your content is successful, but before taking on this venture, make sure you are prepared for the potential costs and risks.

The Tips For Creating A Blog Or Youtube Channel As A Passive Income

Idea

The success of Create a blog or YouTube channel as a passive income idea depends on understanding the key elements of content creation, audience engagement, and monetization.

First, you must have an idea for your blog or YouTube channel that will be interesting to people and provide value to them. Next, you need to research the topics that your audience is interested in and make sure you create content around those subjects. Finally, create a strategy for how often you are going to post or upload videos, as well as what type of content you will be sharing.

The next step is to engage with your audiences on both platforms. This can be done by responding to comments on your posts and videos and actively engaging with users on social media. The more active you are in responding to your audience's questions, the more likely people will be to keep returning for new content.

Finally, Creating a blog or YouTube channel is an important part of making it a passive income idea. There are multiple ways to monetize, such as through advertising, affiliate programs, sponsorships, or even selling products. You have to research what will be the most profitable for your niche and if it is something that aligns with your message and mission.

Advertise On Your Car

Advertise on your car is a great way to make some extra money and get your name out there. Wrapping your car with an advertisement is a relatively simple process that can be quite lucrative, depending on the company or product you are advertising.

In order to Advertise on your car, the first step is finding a company or organization interested in paying for the advertising space. There are a few different ways to do this, such as using online databases that list companies looking for car advertising or searching out local businesses and organizations interested in advertising your car. Once you have found a suitable organization, it is important to make sure the advertisement you agree upon meets all of their needs and specifications.

Once you have a contract in place, the next step is to find a wrap installation company. This is an important step as it ensures that your advertisement will be correctly applied and installed on your car. Most companies will use 3M vinyl wrapping materials which are both durable and attractive. The most common types of vinyl used for Advertise on your car are perforated window films, full wrap films, and cut-vinyl graphics.

Once the Advertise on your car has been installed correctly, it is important to take care of the advertisement. Regularly washing and waxing your car will help keep the advertisement in good condition for a longer period of time. Additionally, it is important to follow the company or organization's instructions regarding the advertisement and not remove or alter the Advertise on your car before the end of its contract.

What Are The Steps For Starting Advertise On Your Car

1. Choose Your Advertiser: First, choose the advertiser you would like to work with. Research potential advertisers to find one that best fits your needs and budget. Be sure to read any contracts thoroughly before signing.

2. Prepare Your Ad: Once you've selected an advertiser, it's time to design your ad. Consider the size, shape, and placement of your advertisement. Your ad should also be eye-catching and creative in order to stand out from other ads.

3. Apply Ad To Vehicle: After you have agreed upon an advertiser and created a design for your ad, it's time to apply it to your vehicle. You can either hire a professional to apply the ad or do it yourself.

Adhesive vinyl is the most common material used for vehicle advertising.

4. Advertise: After your advertisement has been applied, it's time to start advertising. Promote your vehicle on social media and other platforms to draw attention to your business.

5. Collect Payment: Once you've successfully made a few sales, it's time to collect payment. Advertisers typically pay for the ads on a monthly or quarterly basis. Be sure to keep track of all payments so that you can accurately report them to the IRS.

The Advantage Of Advertising On Your Car

Advertise on your car is that it offers a cost-effective way to get your message out there. Ad space on cars is typically much cheaper than traditional advertising methods, like radio or television ads. Additionally, car advertisements can reach more people, since they are often seen in different cities and states. Car wraps also offer an eye-catching way to showcase your brand and bring attention to your business. Advertisers can use graphics, logos, and slogans to create an eye-catching display that will grab the attention of potential customers. Advertisements on cars also last longer than other forms of advertising, since they are less likely to be removed or replaced by someone else's ad. This means that advertisers can get more value out of their investment, since they don't have to keep paying for a new ad every few months. Advertising on cars can also be used to promote special events or deals, allowing businesses to reach more people. As a result, advertisements on cars are becoming increasingly popular and can be an effective way to grow your business.

The Disadvantage Of Advertising On Your Car

Advertise on your car is that you may not have much control over the type of ads that are placed on your vehicle. Advertisers may place advertisements for products or services that you do not endorse or support, which can be embarrassing and damaging to your reputation. Additionally, you will likely be responsible for any damages to your car caused by the ad placement, such as scratches or paint damage. Advertisements can also be a distraction while driving, which can lead to safety hazards and costly accidents. Furthermore, it can be quite expensive to have can be quite expensive your car wrapped with advertisements, so you may not make much money from the program in the end. Finally, if you decide to cancel the program before the contract ends, you may still be required to pay the total amount even if you no longer have the advertisement on your car. Therefore, advertising on your car may not be a viable option for many people, so it is important to research all of your options before making a decision.

The Tips For Advertising On Your Car

Advertising on your car can be a great way to increase your visibility and gain more exposure for your business. However, it is important to do it right in order to maximize the benefits and ensure you don't create any damage or harm to your vehicle. Here are some tips for advertising on your car:

1. Choose well-designed graphics. Make sure your ad graphics are eye-catching, professional, and accurately represent your company.

2. Adhere to the law. Be sure to check local laws for any restrictions on advertising on cars in your area.

3. Prepare your car properly. Clean and wax the surface of your car before applying the decals. Make sure it is completely dry before applying the decals to ensure they stick properly.

4. Protect your car. Use a clear coat sealer over the decals to protect them from weathering and make them last longer.

5. Monitor your ads closely. Check your vehicle frequently for signs of wear and tear and repair any damage quickly.

By following these tips, you can effectively advertise on your car and take advantage of the benefits that come with it. So advertise wisely and reap the rewards!

In conclusion, Advertise on your car can be a great opportunity but it is important to consider the potential drawbacks before committing. For example, advertisers may place ads that do not reflect your own beliefs, you may be responsible for any damages caused by the placement of ads, and it can be expensive. Therefore, advertising on your car should only be considered after careful research and consideration of all possible risks.

Create An App

Create an app is a great way to bring your ideas to life. The possibilities are endless, from turning your creative concepts into reality to reaching more customers. But before you begin the app development process, it's important to understand the steps involved and what is required for a successful launch.

The first step in creating an app involves deciding on the type of application you would like to create. This could be a mobile application, a web-based application or a combination of the two. Next, it is important to determine the platform you plan to develop for and research the best development tools available.

Once you have chosen your platform, it is time to design and develop your app. You will need to plan out the features and functionality, determine the user interface, create a database structure or any other back-end systems, build the code for your app and test your application. You may also need to research third-party services and APIs that you could use to enhance your app's capabilities.

The next step is to launch your application onto the appropriate platform. Depending on your chosen platform, this can be done through an app store or other distribution channel. You will need to ensure that your app is optimised correctly to ensure visibility in the marketplace and create marketing materials to promote its launch.

Finally, you must maintain your application after launch by releasing updates and monitoring user feedback. This will help you ensure that your app performs optimally and engages users.

Creating an app can be a rewarding experience if done properly, but it also requires attention to detail and dedicated effort. Following these steps will help you ensure your project is successful and launch the best possible application.

Advantages Of Creating An App

Creating an app can offer numerous advantages. It allows businesses to provide their customers with a convenient way of accessing their services and products, as well as staying up-to-date on the latest news and updates. An app also provides an easy platform for customer feedback, allowing businesses to make improvements based on user opinions. Additionally, creating an app increases visibility, as it can be used to promote a business and draw in new customers. Finally, an app can help businesses streamline their operations, saving time and money by automating notifications and order tracking tasks. All of these advantages make creating an app a great way for businesses to stay ahead of the competition.

It is also important to note that creating an app does not necessarily have to be a complex and expensive process. Many low-cost options are now available, such as software development kits (SDKs) and mobile application development frameworks (MADFs). These options can help businesses create an app without breaking the bank.

Overall, creating an app can be a great way for

businesses to reach more customers, save time and money, and keep up with the competition. With the right tools and strategies, creating an app can be a cost-effective way for businesses to take their operations to the next level.

Additionally, Creating an app can be a powerful marketing tool and help businesses stand out from their competition. It gives businesses the ability to reach more potential customers and provides a platform for creating engaging content that engages users and encourages conversion. App content such as games, interactive videos, coupons, and notifications can help businesses boost engagement, increase sales and revenue, and engage customers on a deeper level. Apps also provide an easy way for customers to give feedback, allowing businesses to respond quickly to their needs. Creating an app is an invaluable tool in any modern business's arsenal.

The Disadvantages Of Creating An App

Creating an app is not without its drawbacks. It can be a costly and time-consuming process, especially for those who don't have experience in web development or coding. Additionally, there's the risk of compatibility issues that could render the app unusable on certain devices or operating systems. Apps also require regular maintenance and updates to ensure they remain relevant and functional. Once an app is released, fixing errors or addressing customer complaints can be difficult. Finally, the success of an app relies heavily on effective marketing and promotion, which requires effort and dedication. As such, Creating an App is not without its risks and complexities.

Nevertheless, Create an App can prove to be a powerful and effective tool when executed properly. It can help businesses reach a large audience, reduce costs and increase customer engagement. With the right strategy, Creating an App can help an organisation stand out and stay ahead of the competition. But before committing to Creating an App, it's important to have a clear plan and budget in place. Doing this can help ensure the success of Creating an App rather than becoming a costly mistake.

Tips For Creating An App

1. Create a clear concept: It's important to know what your app will do and how it will benefit users. Create a detailed description of the features and functionality you want your app to have, as this will help guide the development process.

2. Identify your target audience: Knowing who you are building the app for is essential in order to create something that meets their needs. Research what other apps exist in your space, and think

about what features and experiences can appeal to your target user base.

3. Create an engaging design: Create a visual language that resonates with your users and reflects the overall theme of your app. This should also include how you want to structure the user experience and how you'd like to organize all of the content for easy navigation.

4. Consider the technical aspects: Create a plan for how to code and develop your app. Think about whether you're using an existing platform or if you need to develop something from scratch, as well as which device platforms you want to build for (iOS, Android, etc.).

5. Test it out: Create a prototype of your app and test it on different devices. This will allow you to tweak any issues as well as get feedback from potential users before launching the final version.

6. Create an action plan: Create a timeline for each step of the development process, including launch dates for beta versions and the final launch date. Create a budget and figure out how you're going to market your app.

Creating an app may seem daunting at first, but by taking it one step at a time and having a clear vision of what you want the end product to look like, you can create something both useful and successful. With some research and planning, anyone can create an app that meets the needs of their target audience.

CHAPER 10 : FREELANCE

Teach online courses

Teaching online courses as a passive income idea is an increasingly popular way to make money from home. With the rise of digital technology, creating and offering high-quality course content is easier than ever. Whether you are an expert on a particular topic or have a wide range of knowledge in different areas, there are many opportunities open to you for teaching online courses.

The key to success is to create engaging content that provides value to students and helps them learn the material. You can monetize your courses by charging a fee for access or offering them free with supplemental materials available as an upsell. You can also use other methods, such as affiliate links or even sponsorships, to make additional money.

When creating courses, consider the needs and interests of your target audience. Ensure to provide detailed information on topics and include plenty of resources for students to explore further. Additionally, you can use online tools such as webinars, forums and email campaigns to engage with learners.

Teaching online courses is a great way to make money while helping others learn new skills. With high-quality content and a structured approach, you can create courses that appeal to the right people and help you generate a steady income stream.

What Are The Steps For Starting Teach Online Courses?

Starting to Teach online courses can be a great way to earn passive income. Here are some steps you need to take in order to get started:

1. Determine what course topics you will teach. This is important as it will help ensure that your teaching materials are relevant and engaging for your students. Next, brainstorm potential ideas

and consider your areas of expertise.

2. Develop a curriculum and materials that you can use to teach the course. You will need to create lesson plans, assignments and activities that align with your chosen topic. Additionally, you should include any supplemental videos, readings or other resources that will be helpful for your students in understanding the content better.

3. Find a platform to host your course materials. Many online platforms are available for hosting teaching online courses, such as Udemy and Coursera. Research different options and decide which one will best suit your Teach online course needs.

4. Promote your Teach online course. Once you have developed the content for your Teach online course, you need to ensure that people know about it. Consider creating a website for the Teach online course and taking advantage of social media platforms like Facebook and Instagram to advertise your Teach online course. Additionally, you may want to consider paid advertising options such as Google Ads or LinkedIn Ads to get more eyes on your Teach online course.

5. Monitor and update your Teach online course as needed. As you Teach online courses, you may need to make adjustments to your curriculum or other aspects of the Teach online course to ensure that your students are getting the most out of

it. Additionally, don't forget to regularly check in with your students for feedback about their experience.

The Advantage Of Teaching Online Courses

is that it can be a great source of passive income. You can create courses or tutorials and sell them to students worldwide, allowing you to earn additional money while still focusing on your current job or other business ventures. Teaching online courses also gives you access to an international market, allowing you to reach more potential customers than you would if you were teaching in person. You can also create courses that are tailored to specific needs, meaning you can focus on a particular topic or skill set that is in demand. Teaching online courses also allows you to work from home or any other location with an internet connection, allowing the flexibility and convenience of working whenever and wherever you choose. Finally, Teaching online courses is a great way to share your expertise and knowledge, while also connecting with others who may be interested in the same topic. By teaching online courses, you can make an impact on people's lives and help them learn something new.

The Disadvantage Of Teaching Online

Courses

is you will have to put a lot of effort into creating and marketing your course. You'll need to research the audience, create materials, and build an online platform. Additionally, you must have the necessary technical knowledge to deliver the course content. Finally, you must invest time and money in marketing your course to get it out there and attract students. This could mean spending a lot of money on online advertising and having to create an effective sales funnel. All of this requires time and effort, which can be difficult if you don't have the right resources or experience. Additionally, depending on the type, of course, you are offering, it may not yield enough revenue to sustain your business. As such, Teach online courses can be very time- and money-consuming. It's important to remember that teaching online courses may not be the most suitable option if you are looking to make extra money with minimal effort.

Tips For Teaching Online Courses

1. Know Your Audience: Before you begin to create an online course, be sure to have a clear understanding of who your target audience is. Knowing your students' age group, education level and interests will help guide the content you

create.

2. Create Engaging Content: To keep students engaged and interested in your online course, you need to create relevant and engaging content. Use visuals, audio and video to supplement your material and make it more interesting for your students.

3. Utilize Different Platforms: In addition to traditional video lectures, consider using different platforms such as quizzes, forums or even hands-on activities to keep your students engaged. Using different platforms can provide a more interactive and dynamic learning experience for your students.

4. Monitor Progress: Keeping track of your student's progress is another way to ensure they are staying on track with their learning objectives. Set up regular check-ins to gauge understanding and offer feedback as needed.

5. Promote Your Course: After you have created your course, be sure to promote it to reach potential students. Utilize social media platforms and other online tools to spread the word about your course.

In conclusion, Teaching online courses is an excellent passive income opportunity that offers flexibility, global reach, and the potential to help others learn and grow. Teach online courses are worth considering if you are looking for ways to generate additional income or share your knowledge with the world.

Record Audiobooks

Record audiobooks are an easy way to make passive income. You can record audiobooks for a variety of different genres and topics, such as fiction, non-fiction, biographies, textbooks and more. It doesn't require any special equipment either—all you need is a good quality microphone and recording software. Recordings are usually done in your home so that you can work at your own pace and schedule.

After recording the audiobook, you'll need to edit it and clean up any background noise or other imperfections to ensure it meets the publisher's or client's standards. Once that's done, the audiobook is ready for distribution online.

What Are The Steps For Starting To Record Audiobooks?

Recording audiobooks is a great way to make passive income while doing something you love. Here are the steps to get started:

1. Choose your subject matter: Do some research and decide what type of audiobooks you want to

record. This could be anything from fiction, non-fiction, children's books, and more.

2. Get the rights: If you plan to record a book that is not in the public domain, you will need to get permission from the copyright holder (often referred to as 'licensing'). This can be done through traditional publishing houses or independent authors/publishers.

3. Record your audiobook: Record your audiobook in a professional studio or use home recording equipment. Be sure to keep track of your recording sessions and take regular breaks.

4. Edit and master the audiobook: Clean up any errors through editing software, add sound effects if desired, and edit for overall quality.

5. Distribute your book: Once you've finished recording and mastering your audiobook, you can distribute it through various platforms like Audible, iTunes, and Google Play.

Advantage Of Record Audiobooks

Recording audiobooks is a great way to generate passive income and make your voice heard. It allows you to build your own brand, showcase your talents, and build an audience of loyal followers. Recordings can be sold online, allowing for a much wider reach than simply selling physical copies in stores. Additionally, it's easier for listeners to access your work, with audiobooks being available on platforms like Audible, Amazon and iTunes. Recordings can also be used to promote authors and publishers, providing increased exposure and sales potential for their works. Recordings are also cheaper to produce than physical copies, making them a more cost-effective option for those who want to make some extra money while showcasing their vocal talents. Additionally, recording audiobooks can be incredibly rewarding and is a great way to hone your craft as a voice actor or narrator. As you advance in the field, you will gain more experience that will help you create higher-quality recordings and increase your visibility.

The Disadvantage Of Record Audiobooks

One disadvantage of recording audiobooks is that the process can take a lot of time and effort. This is especially true if you are unfamiliar with the audio equipment and software required to record, edit, and produce a professional-sounding product. Additionally, depending on the book's length, it could take days or even weeks to finish recording and to edit the audiobook. Furthermore, there is a cost associated with purchasing the necessary equipment and software needed to record an audiobook, which can add up quickly. Last but not least, if you are producing your own audiobooks for sale, then you need to have some knowledge of copyright law to ensure that you are not infringing on any existing copyrights. Therefore, recording audiobooks is not a task that should be taken lightly and requires quite a bit of thought and effort before jumping into the project.

Tips For Record Audiobooks

1. Start by finding the right book. Choose a book that you are comfortable with and can identify with and bring to life in an audio format.

2. Record the book bit by bit, allowing yourself time to stop between chapters and read ahead for context and understanding. This will also help keep your enthusiasm and energy levels up when recording.

3. Record in a quiet, distraction-free environment to get the best quality audio possible. Record in short bursts rather than trying to record large chunks of the book at once.

4. Listen back to your recordings and make sure they are of good enough quality before moving on. Recordings that are too quiet or muffled won't be accepted.

5. Record the book in segments and then edit them together to create the final product. Make

sure to add any additional sound effects or music to enhance the listening experience for your audience.

6. Before submitting your audiobook, make sure you follow the guidelines and instructions provided by the platform you are submitting to. This will ensure that your recordings meet the standards of quality required by the platform.

With these tips, you should be able to create a high-quality audiobook and have fun doing it! Record audiobooks are an enjoyable and rewarding activity.

Overall, Record audiobooks can be a great way to make some extra income or just have an enjoyable hobby, but it is important to understand the time, effort, and money that it can take to produce a quality product. It is also important to ensure that you are familiar with copyright laws to avoid getting yourself into any legal trouble. Record audiobooks can be an enjoyable experience but should only be taken on with careful consideration of the drawbacks involved.

Write A Digital Guide

is an excellent way to make passive income. With the rise of digital content, more and more people are turning to guides as a source of information. By creating and publishing your own guide, you can share your knowledge with others while also making some money on the side.

Creating a digital guide isn't difficult; it just takes some time and effort to create content that will be helpful and engaging for your readers. Here are some tips to get you started:

1. Choose a topic – Pick a subject that interests you and that you know about. Write about something people need help with, such as how to use a product or service, solve a problem, or achieve a goal.

2. Content – Write in-depth, detailed information about your chosen topic. Don't forget to include visuals, such as screenshots and videos, to help illustrate the points you make.

3. Promote your guide – Once you have finished writing it, promote it on social media, in relevant forums, and through other channels, so people can find it.

Creating a digital guide is an excellent way to share your knowledge while also making money. With these tips, you'll be well on your way to creating an engaging and helpful piece of content for others to enjoy.

Royalties

Royalties can be a great passive income stream.

Royalties are payments made to creators of intellectual or artistic property, such as books, music, software and artwork, for the use of their work. Royalties are typically paid at predetermined rates, either one-time or ongoing. Royalties can help create a steady stream of income for those who own creative works such as books, songs, or software. Royalties are usually negotiated in the initial contract between the creator and the user of the work. The royalty rate is typically based on factors such as the market value of the work, the estimated number of users, and potential long-term profitability. Royalties can be a lucrative source of passive income for creators who own the intellectual property rights to a work, either as an individual or through a company. Royalties are typically paid on a quarterly basis and can provide creators with a consistent source of income over time. Royalties can also be used to fund future creative projects, allowing creators to focus on the creation process and not worry about the financial aspect. Royalties have helped countless creators make a living from their creative works, allowing them to create more art and help others do the same. Royalties are an excellent way for creators to monetize their work and generate passive income. They allow people to continue producing art without worrying about how they will make money from it.

What Are The Steps For Starting Royalties As A Passive Income?

The first step to starting Royalties as a passive income is to create an original intellectual property work, such as a book, song, or invention. This will be the basis for your royalty stream. Once you have created the intellectual property, it is important to register it with the appropriate copyright office or patent office. This will ensure you receive the proper legal protection for your work.

The next step is to identify potential royalty streams for your intellectual property. Royalties can be derived from merchandise, book sales, song downloads, and more. Research various outlets and markets that could generate royalties from your intellectual property.

Once you have identified a few sources of potential royalties, securing contracts with those outlets is important. Many of these deals may involve giving up some portion of your royalties in exchange for the right to have your intellectual property sold through their platform and/or provide other services such as marketing and promotion.

Finally, you should consider diversifying your royalty streams by creating additional products or services related to your original intellectual property. This can help minimize any potential losses from a single source while increasing the total amount of royalties you receive.

With these steps in place, Royalties can provide a steady stream of passive income for creative entrepreneurs. They offer an opportunity to make money with minimal effort and time commitment, allowing you to focus on creating more new works. Royalties can also serve as a way to monetize your creative efforts, providing financial security and the potential for long-term residual income.

The Advantage Of Royalties

as a passive income, it can be earned from various sources such as books, music, films, and other forms of intellectual property. Royalties can be earned by the creator of the work or through contracts with companies that license the use of their material for various purposes. Royalties are typically paid out on a regular basis, usually monthly or quarterly, and are typically a percentage of the revenue generated by the use of the material. Royalties can be quite lucrative as they provide a steady stream of income without necessarily requiring daily attention or effort on the creator's part. Royalties are often paid out over years or even decades, providing creators a long-term source of passive income. Royalties are a great way for creators to monetize their work and take advantage of the potential for significant income over time. Royalties can be used to supplement traditional income sources or create an entirely new revenue stream. Ultimately, Royalties allow creators to generate passive income from their work that does not require constant effort and attention. Royalties can be a great way for creators to generate long-term, passive income and turn their creative work into a lucrative business.

The Disadvantage Of Royalties

Royalties are that they can be slow to accumulate. Royalties are based on sales, meaning it takes time for them to become substantial. Royalties also tend to favour those who have already established themselves in their respective fields. It is more difficult for newcomers to reap the benefits of Royalties due to the fact that they may not have as much of an audience or as much of an established presence. Royalties can also be difficult to track and are subject to various fees and commission structures that can eat away at the profits earned. Finally, Royalties require ongoing maintenance in order for them to remain effective. If a creator fails to keep up with the necessary paperwork or if their content becomes outdated, Royalties may be reduced or eliminated. Royalties can also be unpredictable as sales of content can fluctuate over time. This makes Royalties a risky form of passive income and creators need to understand the potential risks before committing to Royalties as their primary source of income.

Tips For Royalties As A Passive Income

Royalties can be an excellent way to generate passive income. Royalties are payments made to individuals or businesses for the use of their property, such as intellectual property, music, artwork and other creative works. Royalties provide revenue over a long period, often with minimal effort on the creator's part. Here are some tips to help you maximize your royalty income:

1. Research Royalties: Start by learning all you can about royalties and how they work. Understand the different types of royalties, including performance and mechanical royalties, and how they are collected and distributed.

2. Create Quality Content: The quality of your content is key to generating royalty income. Make sure you are creating unique, valuable, and appealing content for potential customers.

3. Market Your Content: Once your content is created, it's important to ensure people can find it. Consider different marketing strategies such as search engine optimization (SEO), social media or

advertising to help get your content in front of potential customers.

4. Protect Your Content: Royalties are based on the usage of your property, so it's important to protect it from unauthorized use and piracy. Consult with an intellectual property attorney to discuss your options for legally protecting your work.

5. Track Royalties: Royalties can be difficult to track, so it's important to have a system in place for keeping track of your income. Consider using software or services that can help you manage and monitor your royalty payments.

By following these tips, you can ensure that you make the most out of your royalty income and maximise its potential.

In conclusion, Royalties are an attractive passive income option for some creators, but they can also be difficult to obtain and manage. Royalties require ongoing maintenance to remain effective and may not always provide a steady income stream. Therefore, creators should carefully weigh the potential risks before committing to Royalties as their primary source of income. It is important to understand that Royalties largely depend on the success of one's content and may not always provide a steady income stream. Royalties can, however, be an excellent form of passive income for those who are able to establish themselves successfully in their respective fields. Proper planning and management allow Royalties to be a lucrative source of passive income.

CONCLUSION

Passive income is income that comes from investments or sources that require minimal effort to maintain and generate profits. This type of income usually requires upfront investment but can provide a steady stream of income over time. Examples of passive income include rental properties, dividend stocks, royalties received from selling intellectual property rights, and other investments.

Active income, on the other hand, is income earned through activities or work that are performed on a regular basis. This type of income requires continuous effort and often provides a less reliable source of income when compared to passive income sources. Examples of active income include wages from an employer, freelance services, or self-employment.

The key difference between passive and active incomes is the amount of effort and time that is needed for each type of income. Passive income requires an upfront investment and can provide a steady stream of profits over time, while active income generally requires continuous effort to generate profit. Therefore, it is important to consider both types of income in order to make the most informed decisions about personal finance and investments.

Overall, passive income is a great way to generate long-term profits with minimal effort, while active income can provide a more reliable source of short-term income. When deciding which type of income to pursue, it is important to consider both options and find the one that best suits your needs. By doing this, you will be able to maximize your earning potential and make the most of your finances.

The main takeaway is that it's important to understand the differences between passive income and active income in order to make an informed decision on which type of income you should pursue. Passive income provides a long-term source of profits with minimal effort, while active income requires regular effort but may provide more reliable income in the short-term. Ultimately, it's a personal decision that depends on your individual needs and goals.

Have More Financial Stability is one of the key advantages of passive income ideas. With steady income streams, you can ease your financial stress and enjoy more financial security regardless of how much effort is put in to maintain it.

This could mean having extra funds to cover unexpected expenses or even having enough money to purchase that dream home or car you've been wanting for years. In addition, having more financial stability can provide you with the freedom to pursue other interests and passions without worrying about running out of money. From investing in a new business venture or taking up a hobby, these opportunities become available when a steady income comes in from passive sources.

Passive income is a type of income that does not require direct effort from the individual to generate. A few examples of passive income include rental property investments, royalties from intellectual property or other investments such as stocks and bonds.

Rental Property: Rental properties are an ideal source of passive income because they require minimal upkeep and can provide steady cash flow with little effort. Potential investors can purchase rental properties and then lease them out to tenants, collecting rent payments each month before turning around and reinvesting that money into more rental properties or other investments.

Royalties are an income stream generated when a creative person earns residuals from the sale of their works. This could include books, music, videos, and more. When these works are sold to consumers, the creator earns a percentage of each sale in passive income.

Stocks and Bonds: Investing in stocks and bonds is another way to generate passive income. Investors can purchase stocks and bonds with the intention of holding them for earning dividends or capital gains through appreciation over time.

Real Estate Investing: Another form of passive income is real estate investing. Investors can purchase properties and then rent them out to tenants for a steady stream of passive income. Real estate investments also have the potential for appreciation over time, further increasing the investor's profits.

Online Businesses: An online business is one of the more modern types of passive income. Individuals can create websites, blogs, or e-commerce stores to generate income through advertising or affiliate marketing. This form of passive income requires some initial effort to set up, but once it's running, it can provide a steady stream of passive income without the need for any ongoing maintenance or effort.

MAY I ASK YOU FOR A SMALL FAVOR?

Before you go, please, I need your assistance! In case you like this book, might you be able to please share your opinion on ... and compose a legit review? It will take only one moment for you, yet it will be an extraordinary favour for me. Since I'm not a famous writer, I don't have a large distributing organization supporting me. I read each and every review and hop around with happiness like a little child each time my audience remark on my books and give me their fair criticism! ☺. If you didn't appreciate the book or had an issue with it, kindly get in touch with me via email; ... and reveal how I can improve it.

Made in the USA
Las Vegas, NV
17 September 2023

77749927R00111